LIGHT TRACES

LIGHT TRACES

JOHN SALLIS

Paintings and drawings
by Alejandro A. Vallega

Indiana University Press   Bloomington & Indianapolis

This book is a publication of

INDIANA UNIVERSITY PRESS
Office of Scholarly Publishing
Herman B Wells Library 350
1320 East Tenth Street
Bloomington, Indiana 47405 USA

iupress.indiana.edu

Telephone   800-842-6796
Fax   812-855-7931

♾ The paper used in this publication
meets the minimum requirements of the
American National Standard for Information
Sciences – Permanence of Paper for Printed
Library Materials, ANSI Z39.48–1992.

Manufactured in China

Library of Congress
Cataloging-in-Publication Data

Sallis, John, [date]
    Light traces / John Sallis; paintings
and drawings by Alejandro A. Vallega.
    pages cm. – (Studies in
Continental thought)
    ISBN 978-0-253-01282-1 (pbk. : alk.
paper) – ISBN 978-0-253-01303-3 (ebook)
1. Place (Philosophy) 2. Light. I. Vallega,
Alejandro A., illustrator. II. Title.
    B105.P53S245 2014
    113 – dc23

                                    2013034396

1 2 3 4 5   19 18 17 16 15 14

To live is to behold the light of the sun.

Homer

Contents

Acknowledgments

We are grateful to Sarah Grew for her generosity in providing the photographic images and to Nancy Fedrow for her assistance in preparing the manuscript. We want especially to thank our friend and editor Dee Mortensen for the encouragement and advice she has so generously offered us during our collaboration on this project. Thanks also to Sean Driscoll for editorial assistance.

J. S.
A. V.

LIGHT TRACES

Anagoge

The return of light in spring brings joy and hope to living things. For in one way or another light governs virtually everything of concern to them. It makes visible the things around them; it lets the presence of things and of natural elements be sensed in the most disclosive manner; and thereby it clears the space within which things can be most sensibly encountered and elements such as earth and sky can be revealed in their gigantic expanse. The coming and going of natural light also gives the measure of time, coming to bestow the day, retreating to give way to night. Light also measures out the seasons, not only by its intensity as the sun appears higher or lower in the sky, but also by variations that are not readily expressible in traditional categories: as with the crystal-clear sunlight of certain winter days when the scattered clouds appear in sharpest contour against a sky so blue that it exceeds all that can be said in the word *blue*.

With the new light that marks the arrival of spring and that brings with it the promise of warmth, the threats of winter recede. Fresh growth appears, first as little more than a fine green haze and then in delicate forms that attest to the fecundity of nature, still held in store but portended by these light traces. Now abundant vitality is displayed by all animate creatures. We humans, too, welcome the arrival of spring, not only in our ordinary actions but also in exceptional events such as rites and festivals. For the ancient Athenians festivals were so decisive in marking not only the arrival of seasons but all the months of their lunar calendar that each month literally bore the name of the chief festival celebrated within its time-span.

Yet as it returns, light remains curiously inconspicuous, even more so than the natural finery that its return will eventually release from the things with which nature surrounds us. For quite some time after the winter solstice, we are scarcely aware of the increasing daylight; and it may happen almost suddenly, several weeks later, that we notice the lengthening of the day. It is as if the luminous generosity were effected by stealth.

Light is also inconspicuous in another way, in a way that is itself inconspicuous, hardly noticed at all.

Picture a scene in the forest where sunlight is shining through the branches onto the ground below. There will be areas that are brightly illuminated, others that are shaded, and, as a result, a configuration of light and shadow on the forest floor. There will also be visible illumination on some of the branches above. Yet in the space between the lowest branches and the forest floor, no illumination will be visible. Though light must traverse this space in order to illuminate the ground below, it remains entirely invisible. Only if the space contains particles of dust or a bit of mist or fog—that is, things to be illuminated—does the ray of light become visible. Even on the forest floor what we actually see is not the light itself but the ground illuminated by the light. The light itself, which bestows on things their visibility, remains to this extent invisible. It goes unseen, and yet in connection with what is seen, it displays a trace that is indicative of its effect, of its being operative there at the site of the visible. Unlike an image, in which an aspect of some visible thing is presented, a trace does not present anything; it is, rather, that by which something otherwise concealed, something irreducible to a thing that is present, signals that it is nonetheless operative there in the very thick of visible things.

Of light there are, then, only traces. To turn to the light is to attend to light traces.

In most instances it is also to turn one's gaze upward toward the primary source of light. Accordingly, the turn to the light is linked to the preeminence of the sky, to our affinity with the heights, and to the prospect of ascendancy. In all these inclinations the directive is given by light traces. It is light that traces the upward way, that evokes the aspiration for flight, which, in various metaphorical registers, moves us at the most elemental level. Nothing human goes untouched by this aspiration; nothing is immune to the measure of the upward way, neither to its promise nor to its peril.

Traces are necessarily light. They are, like light itself, free of the weight of things materially present. Even when they are drawn or inscribed and thus transposed into a minimally present double, they retain much of their lightness. The triangle that is drawn in order to facilitate intuition must in effect erase itself in the course of the demonstration it serves. For it is not really an image or picture through which the triangle itself would be presented. Formed by lines that are without width and hence, strictly considered, are invisible, a triangle is itself invisible; and a drawing can be nothing more than a trace serving to bring the figure to light.

Words, too, especially when their saying is most forceful, cease to be mere images of the things to which they refer and of the meanings they express. Above and beyond merely signifying, they come to trace, ever so lightly, the contours and weavings of undivided sense. The endless aporias that result from the failure to grant this excess belonging to speech were indeed already catalogued, in comical fashion, in an ancient dialogue named for one who is reputed finally to have given up speaking entirely and only to have resorted to the merest gestures.

Yet what is perhaps most remarkable is the way in which the artist can let traces such as those of light become visible without violating their character as traces. Such is the gift of the artist: to let the trace present itself through the image, to render the invisible visible in a way that, at once, preserves its invisibility.

·   ·   ·   ·

Since the cycle of light's coming and going defines the course of the year, these texts, designed as light inscriptions, also follow this course; but, like the ancient Roman calendar, they proceed from the time of the light's return in spring to that of its retreat in the depth of winter. Yet light's comings and goings leave different traces, depending on the terrain where they are drawn. On a Pacific island or an Aegean site, in a capital city or high in the Alps, at the sea or in the forest–in each place the traces not only are different but also serve to disclose in multiple, incomparable ways the workings of light and the measuring out of time. To inscribe such elemental interweavings of luminosity, time, and place is the intent of the following series of light traces.

The images in this volume are not meant as illustrations of the text; they were specially conceived as graphic articulations of light, another language, meant to enter into dialogue with the text. Also, the drawings and paintings are not representations of light. The light traces occur in the play of line, color, chiaroscuro, textures, and materials.

1
Clouds

Oahu
Hawai'i

March

Clouds are little more than traces of light. On sunny days when only a
few are scattered about the sky, the clouds appear to amplify the light,
all the more so if they are of the white, voluminous sort. Because they
are hardly distinguishable from the light, it is as if they bestowed their
whiteness on the purely white, but invisible, light itself, by this means
endowing it with perceptible form, rendering it visible. At dawn and dusk
and also when configured in certain ways, they can give the light a vari-
ety of shades, letting it reflect the colors assumed by the rising or setting
sun. These brilliant colors may, in turn, be reflected across the surface of
the sea, endowing the sea with colors quite other than its own, colors that
it will retain for some time even after the sun has sunk below the horizon
or risen to the height at which it becomes the clear, daytime sun.

 Clouds are among the lightest of traces because they are insubstantial; though not quite immaterial, they are perfect semblances of

immateriality. They can fill the otherwise invisible air with visibility while simultaneously concealing more substantial things. When surrounded by low-lying clouds in the mountains, we witness such an exchange between the visible and the invisible: the massive stone face of the adjacent mountain recedes from view while the surrounding space garners an opaque visibility. Walking freely, if somewhat blindly, across such a site, passing through patches of unsubstantial cloud without encountering the slightest resistance, we observe that, while it obscures the source of light, the cloud renders the light visible; it provides a visible trace unlike any to be seen in the purely transparent air of a cloudless day.

Clouds can gather or obstruct light in such a way as to be portentous. Dark clouds may gather in the distance in a manner that announces unmistakably the imminent arrival of a thunderstorm and thus prompts an interruption of the everyday course of things as living creatures, ourselves included, seek shelter. At other times it may happen that the cloud cover that remains even after the heavy rain has ended finally begins to break up, the clouds gradually dispersing so as to let sunlight reappear and thus to announce the return of fair conditions. In such happenings the light traces produced through the interactions of sunlight and clouds are indicative; they announce something to come, yet they do so in a way that differs utterly from the way in which words signify. To such natural indications even animate beings bereft of language are sensitive. On the other hand, those with speech have never ceased being tempted to suppose that speech is sustained by such natural indications, that despite the conventionality and diversity of languages, there is a–perhaps concealed–affinity between words and things. It is as if there belonged to speech – or to the bearing of those who speak – an aspiration to natural speech, to a speech that would indicate things by nature.

.   .   .   .

The day had in fact been almost cloudless until midafternoon. But then, dark rain clouds blew in over the island. The blackest of them gradually descended until, like a thick veil, it entirely enshrouded the low mountain that lay just down the beach from the covering where I took shelter. Finally, when the black cloud had reached the ground, it was as if the mountain had entirely vanished without leaving the slightest trace. The concealment was so complete that it was itself concealed. So concealed was the concealment that, had I not already known of its presence, I would not have had even the slightest suspicion that the mountain was there.

The clouds proved to be much more threatening than what they portended. Only a few large raindrops fell, and then, very soon, the first sign of clearing appeared.

Far out at sea the sun broke through the clouds, and there along a stretch of the horizon – indeed forming a stretch of the horizon – was a broad band of pure light shining with such intensity that I could not but turn my eyes away after just a moment. It was as if the clouds had released the light and, because they were themselves so dark, had endowed it with the most extreme luminosity, calling on the sea to mirror the light, to let the intense light be traced. There on the surface of the sea, at the horizon, it shone so brilliantly, with such intensity, that it bordered on being invisible – almost as the sun, because of the brilliance of its shining, resists direct vision, offering only a glance.

After a while the band of light began to fade a bit, though still clinging to the horizon. Eventually other, less brilliant spots began to appear on the water as the sun broke more and more through the clouds. The entire scene began to settle back into its usual, everyday appearance. Yet I continued to marvel at what I had observed: how the brilliant light trace at the horizon had polarized and indeed transformed the entire scene so suddenly and yet so briefly. Not even the sight from the plane at 38,000 feet – as I journeyed onward the following day – the sight of the vast field of voluminous clouds, manifestly insubstantial as nonetheless they gathered the light, could rival the exchange I had witnessed between the dark clouds, the open sea, and the brilliant light.

Untitled
(Oil and pencil on
paper), 18×24 in.

2
Caves

Kaua'i
Hawai'i

April

There are opposites that are said and opposites that are seen. When opposites that have been said come to be seen, they inevitably prove to be less opposed than they were said to be. The sky above is no mere opposite of the earth below; rather, they are also bound together, encompassing the space in which nearly everything of concern to humans appears. Day and night, determined primarily by the presence or absence of sunlight, not only are bound by their sequential occurrence but also display, each in its own way, a certain play of light. No matter how brilliantly illuminated it may be, no daytime scene is totally without its shadows. Only rarely, if ever, is the night completely dark; and even then, light can always be kindled.

So it is, also, with the relation between the open air, which can be filled with radiant sunlight, and the dark sea, which keeps its depths withdrawn from the light. So it is, to a greater degree, with the relation of the open air to the compact, closed-off earth. In whatever ways they may be bound together, nothing both conjoins and distinguishes them more decisively than their peculiar reception of light. Wherever either extends into the other, there is a site that displays the reception and play of light in an exemplary way.

·   ·   ·   ·

Both kinds of sites can be seen on Kaua'i. Off the east coast of the island, not far from shore, a dome-shaped mass of rock protrudes into the open air. Despite its dull earthen color, it shares in the brilliant illumination that the tropical sun spreads over everything. Yet it receives the sunlight only on its surface, casting much of it back, attesting in this way to its earthen character, its density, its closedness. In this manner it is set entirely apart from the surrounding sea, which to some extent admits the sunlight, letting it penetrate the surface and displaying it in the expanse of deep, rich blueness.

Caves, on the other hand, extend from the open air into the earth, penetrating into the interior of the hill or mountain in which they are set. They violate the seal, opening the dense, spaceless interior, carving out a space, a void within the solid rock. Caves open out the interior so as to make visible what would otherwise never be seen, could indeed not be seen. Only in caves does one get a glimpse of the otherwise invisible interior of a hill or mountain.

On the wild northern coast of Kaua'i there are two very remarkable caves. The area in which they are situated resembles a rain forest, in stark contrast to the sun-drenched, palm tree–studded beaches on the southern coast. In this area the terrain is rough. Just past the caves the road swings out to a small beach (Kē'ē Beach) where it comes abruptly to an end; beyond that point, for many miles around the Nāpali Coast, which forms the northwest corner of the island, there are only steep mountainsides plunging downward to the sea.

The cave nearest the end of the road is the Waikanaloa Wet Cave. Advancing down a slight incline, one comes to the opening of the cave. There at the opening one looks out across a black pool that stretches on into the cave. In the dim light some fifty feet or so into the cave, a wall of stone can be seen extending across the breadth of the cave; there, barely discernible, the water branches off in almost opposite directions. Yet it is not the dark interior of the cave that is most remarkable but rather the more open area near the mouth. One could readily imagine that some ancient giant or titan had ripped open this huge, gaping hole in the side of the mountain. Here there are no smooth, polished stone surfaces but only sharp, pointed shards, protrusions of stone that attest to the very stoniness of the mountain. The site is one where the mountain shows what it is, where it makes manifest that its interior is just the same stone as its surface. Yet here near the opening the sharp, protruding stone assumes a kind of protoform and in this way obtrudes in its stony presence, even though form is what earth in its elemental character lacks almost entirely.

The other cave, the Maninholo Dry Cave, is quite different. It is almost rectangular in shape, its sides curving only slightly. Its height is as if proportioned to the height of humans, only a few feet higher. On entering it, one could readily imagine that one is walking into a large hall. Though naturally the light grows dimmer as one proceeds toward the back wall, it remains sufficient for seeing clearly even the back wall and for ascertaining that the cave has no further extensions beyond its rectangular space. Yet what is genuinely astonishing is the sight one beholds when, having walked almost to the back wall of the cave, one suddenly turns around and looks back at the entrance. What can then be seen just outside the cave appears framed, almost like a picture, by the contour of the opening; and, within this frame, it appears with a remarkable, stark brilliance, quite different from the appearance when seen from the entrance. The withdrawal of vision, the retreat into the dim light of the cave, has the effect of enhancing the appearing of things, of bringing them to shine more luminously.

Coming to see things in their most radiant shining may well require, for humans, retreating also into the obscurity of something like a cave, especially if, for us, darkness always belongs also with the light that brings illumination. Since indeed we can no more see in pure light than in pure darkness, it is little wonder that the image of a cave has acquired such metaphorical value that the very course prescribed for humans is bound to this representation. And yet, neither retreat nor escape suffices alone for the illumination to which humans are disposed. It is required also, as the ancient image attests, that we turn to the light.

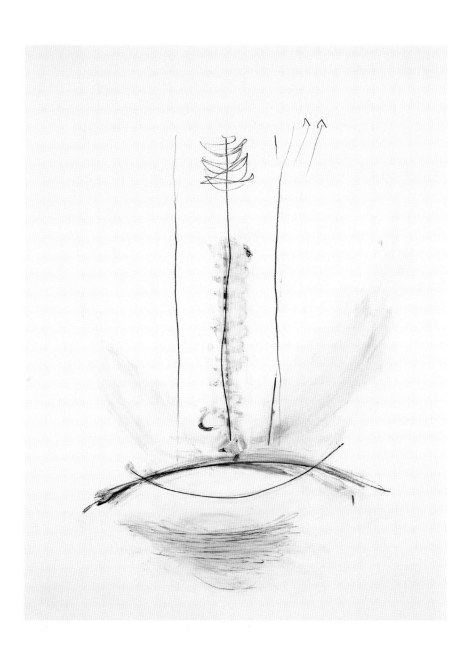

Spring I
(Oil and pencil on
paper), 18×24 in.

Spring II
(Oil and pencil on
paper), 18×24 in.

3
Exorbitant
Points

Near Patras
Peloponnisos

May

Though broader than a great river, the Bay of Corinth flows gently, as if it were a vast lake with no opening onto the sea. It sets the Peloponnisos apart from the rest of Greece. Indeed, together with the Saronic Bay, it divides the entire country into two parts, bridged only by the isthmus running from Corinth across into Attica. Bordered on the east by the isthmus and the city of Corinth, it extends westward and slightly to the north until, as it approaches Patras, it reaches its narrowest point. This is the point where today an ultramodern bridge has been erected across the bay, a technical counterpart to the natural bridge at the other end of the bay. As Athenian hoplites once marched to battle across the isthmus, now on the other bridge automobiles cross swiftly from one side to the other. As the bay extends on past Patras, it broadens out again and soon heads for the open sea that separates the Peloponnisos from the islands of Kephalonia and Ithaca. Beyond the islands lies the Ionian Sea.

If one looks across the bay from the Peloponnisian side, one soon discovers that the broad sweep of the spectacle displays both lineation and punctuation. These features are allied with the attractive power by which the aquatic surface gathers around itself the entire scene, composing the landscape, while at the same time collecting, intensifying, reflecting, and spreading the sunlight that bathes the scene. Opening to the light, vision retraces the lines drawn by nature across the scene and remarks their points of intersection.

The scene leaves its traces on all the senses, not just individually but in such a way that each sense crosses over to the others, effacing their difference. Vision is paired with listening; they flow together to such an extent that the sight of the water's expansive surface becomes almost indistinguishable from the recurrent sound of the waves gently lapping onto the beach. In turn, the sound of the waves as they break along the shoreline intermingles with the sight of the occasional whitecap. The fresh scent of the sea air and the feel of the light breeze wafting from the water, perhaps even an imagined sense of the briny taste of the water–all that the senses offer is gathered as into a single, yet manifold perception, as if pointing back toward a sense anterior to the senses.

Off to the left where, beyond Patras, the bay broadens out again and heads westward toward the open sea, no land can be seen. The surface of the water stretches on and on, as if it were a kind of palpable, sensuous infinite, limited only by the horizon. Though the horizon appears as a line separating, while also joining, sea and sky, its appearance could not be more paradoxical, more counter to the usual categories and oppositions by which appearances in nature are proportioned to our understanding. The appearance of the horizon is neither a mere illusion of something simply not there nor a revelation of something actually present in or behind the appearance. The horizon is not even present in the manner characteristic of elements such as the sea and the earth. Rather, it appears solely as a limit, indeed as a limit that never actually limits, that never sets a limit in place; for, if approached, it recedes, and it resists to the end being transformed from a mere limit into something that limits. As long as land does not come into view there in the distance so as to set a limit, the horizon lets the peculiar infinity of the sea remain intact.

Yet land does come into view if one turns one's glance back slightly to the right, still facing in the general direction of the open sea. It is a thin strip of land running along the horizon, expanding the line into a narrow band. Still farther to the right, almost directly across the bay, a mountain of bare stone protrudes abruptly from the sea, rising almost vertically to nearly half its full height before beginning to curve back in the direction of the horizontal; thus the top of the mountain is rounded off, and its outline becomes almost symmetrical.

It is as if the scene had been staged, fabricated by some monstrous technology, rather than composed by nature. In the scene there is nothing more remarkable than the singular point to which the thin strip of land to the left directs our vision like an arrow drawn across the water in the direction of this point. At this point earth, sea, and sky meet. Here there is a confluence of these elements, not as in a thunderstorm where rain, wind, thunder, and lightning are mixed together, but rather in such a way that each element remains distinct and retains its own character, while, nonetheless, coming together with the others at this point. The pure diurnal sky displays a narrow band of wispy clouds just above the horizon, rendering all the more conspicuous this paradoxical line where the sky meets the sea. The surface of the sea is textured by its gentle purling; the ripples spread across its expanse, endowing the wind with visibility, translating its invisible flow into a visible patterning; their spread also lays out an image of time itself, which, at least since antiquity, has never ceased being represented by the flow of natural waters. Precisely at the point where the stone erupts from the sea, all these elements come together, while their differences remain: the absolutely immobile sky, textured by clouds, punctuated by the very source of light; the sea with its gentle flow and its spread of ripples; the wind to which this spread gives visible testimony; the sheer, unyielding stone of the mountain, the earth jutting up skyward, its contour traced against the sky. In a sense it is a simple vision, a vision that, gathering the elements, comes to focus on this singular point, lets them be gathered around it. The vision is preeminently elemental, a vision for which what comes to light are the elements and not mere things. Yet also, it is a vision in which, drawn into the distance, vision now leaps beyond its comingling with the other senses, reasserting its superiority as the sense of distance.

.   .   .   .

I had come to Patras to speak about the exorbitant, about what lies outside the orbit in which our usual thinking about nature circulates. Nothing could have displayed the exorbitant logic of the elements more powerfully than this spectacle of their gathering. What seemed most remarkable was that I had come upon this display of the exorbitant precisely in Greece. For it is from Greek thought that our usual thinking about nature draws nearly all its resources and indeed its very bounds and measure. The display of nature exceeding such bounds and measure could not, then, but prompt an intimation of a more decisive, indeed exorbitant thinking that was not alien to the Greeks.

4
Poseidon

Sounion
Attica

May

Its place is other, utterly so. Its remoteness is so unyielding that any attempt to measure its distance from anything familiar could only have the effect of setting it still more insistently apart. Yet precisely as a place of such alterity, this site is most impressive to behold in its sheer presence. Perfectly framed by sea and sky, as if raised by the earth itself up out of the intensely blue surface of the Aegean, the site belongs uniquely to these elements. Even in antiquity, indeed even before the magnificent temple was erected there, travelers of many sorts were attracted. Today, in still greater numbers, tourists come with cameras in hand to have a look at this remarkable site and to capture its image. Yet the distraction is no more than momentary. As soon as one is again alone in what remains of the sacred precinct, from the moment when solitude returns and there is left only these stones shining there amidst the elements, the utter strangeness of the site is again announced in the silence that surrounds.

What remains at this site comes from another world, from what we call – already beginning to mediate, to break down the difference – Greek antiquity. Yet, precisely in its otherness, this world is the origin of origins, the absolutely archaic. It first released all that was to come: the course of what came to constitute the West, and now the global figure into which those lines have extended. It is an origin that, from the beginning, continued to animate what it had released, coming, to this extent, always from the future. Thus its remoteness is irreducible to mere pastness; and even now, in the wake of closure, it summons from beyond. It is an origin thus withdrawn into both past and future, hence doubly remote from the present, so that the remains of it that are now still to be seen – as in the stones preserved at this site – cannot but appear utterly strange. The place is, at once, displaced, almost as into a void, and yet it is set firmly on the earth, shining before our eyes in the brilliant Greek sunlight. Its conjunction of consummate presence and staunch remoteness, of stark manifestness and utter strangeness, is cast in the light itself, in the almost blinding intensity of its illumination.

A portion of the wall that once surrounded the sacred precinct is still to be seen. Little remains, however, of the marble-covered propylaea through which one would have entered the enclosure. The location is marked by an inscription – recent, no doubt – on a slab of marble; but the remains are meager, merely three sections of a column and a few other slabs. An inscription also marks the location of the large stoa that extended laterally from the propylaea; but here, too, very little remains, only the stylobates or bases of five columns. Even as one is present at the very spot where the propylaea and the stoa once stood, the visible traces that remain can sustain only a vague image of how these would have looked: that the propylaea, as the opening to the temple, would have been especially magnificent and that the marble surfaces of both structures would have shined luminously.

At such a site where one is faced with ruins, what is called forth is never just pure phantasy, not even just phantasy sustained by memory of images previously seen or of familiar descriptions. Rather, if one is intent on envisaging, to the extent possible, what once stood at this site, then the imagining called for will be such as to circulate between the visibly present ruins and an image of the ancient structure, hovering between these, letting each inform the other.

But it is in face of the ruins of the temple itself that imagination is sustained and hence soars. These ruins are extensive enough and sufficiently well preserved that from them alone many features of the temple are evident. The columns display its Doric order, and their configuration indicates that the temple was peripteral. The majority of the columns along the longer sides of the temple are still standing: nine on the more seaward, southern side, five (along with a couple of sections of another) on the other side. The marble, which came from nearby quarries, is more purely white than that of many other such edifices (such as the Pentelic marble used for the Parthenon); but the material is also softer, and it was presumably in order to strengthen the columns that the architect reduced the fluting from the usual twenty to sixteen. The distinctive radiance with which the stone gives back the light it receives is not unrelated to these features.

On top of the columns, running horizontally, are the epistyles, rectangular blocks on which the superstructure would have rested. On the two shorter sides much less remains. On the eastern side, which would have formed the entrance to the temple, there are one column, the base of another, and two stacks of rectangular blocks, many of them almost cubical. The stacks, which are the same height as the columns, are connected to columns by epistyles. Protrusions from them toward the interior of the temple indicate that these stacks of square blocks form the extremity from which the solid inner walls would have extended; these are the only traces of the inner walls that remain. On the western side of the temple, nothing remains standing.

The blocks that form the base of the edifice are mostly intact: the stylobates, of course, on which the columns rest, but also most of those that would have formed the floor of the chambers. The entire temple is elevated above the surrounding grounds, most conspicuously so on the lower side of the sloping ground, where the base is several meters high and requires for each vertical section eight to ten rectangular blocks.

The promontory on which the temple stands lies at the extremity of the cape of Sounion, which forms the southernmost tip of Attica. The strategic importance that the location had for Athens led to its being fortified in 413 BC, shortly after the magnificent temple had been erected (c. 440 BC) to replace a porous rock temple that after only a few decades had been completely destroyed by the Persians. This very remarkable site is mentioned already in the *Odyssey*. In a passage in the Third Book, Odysseus relates that as he and Menelaus were sailing back from Troy they "came to holy Sounion, the cape of Athens." There Menelaus' steersman Phrontis was slain by unseen arrows of Apollo. To pay full honor to this most excellent of all men in piloting a ship through strong storm winds, Menelaus interrupted their journey at

Sounion and there buried his comrade. Two centuries before the great marble temple came to be erected on the promontory at Sounion, several marble *kouroi* were placed there, presumably as votive offerings whose presence might ensure that sailors passing by would escape what had befallen Phrontis. One such *Kouros of Sounion,* quite well preserved, can be seen in the National Archaeological Museum in Athens.

The temple is placed so as to overlook the sea. From the north side, one looks across an inlet; to the south and the west, one looks out across open sea stretching to the horizon. From the perimeter of the temple, a few paces in any of these directions brings one to the precip- itous edge of the site. One's vision plummets almost straight down to the rocks and the sea far below. Near the rugged shore there are areas where the water is almost emerald green; but as one looks farther out, it is consistently such a deep blue that, at the horizon, the sky appears, by contrast, unusually pale, almost washed-out, by contrast, in turn, with the intense blueness of the sky overhead.

Yet while the presence of the sea is what most decisively deter- mines the character of the site, the history borne by it enlivens that presence. The Homeric passage alone suffices to show that the Greeks experienced that presence, not as totally unreserved exposure to panoptic vision, but rather as harboring also a depth from out of which something barely describable can unaccountably appear and then just as unaccountably–that is, mythically–vanish. The very idiom on which one most readily draws could not be more indicative: presence was experienced as if, like the sea, it withdrew into its depth and as if there were secret inlets, harbors, where things could be hidden away.

What could be more appropriate than the encompassing presence of the sea? For what stands there is a temple of Poseidon, and Poseidon is god of the sea. But what does it mean for a temple, an edifice constructed by humans, to belong to the god? And what does it mean to say that Poseidon is god of the sea? What kind of comportment to the temple and to the sea would be appropriate for the figure that the Greeks called Poseidon? How is it that what once stood at Sounion overlooking the sea and stands there still in ruins can be called a temple of the god of the sea?

At the site there is not only the intense presence of the sea but also an elevation above it. While overlooking the sea, the temple stands at a height befitting a god. It is as if raised from out of the wine-dark sea into the brilliant sunlight above. There, far above the sea, its columns of purely white marble, outlined against the intense blue of the diurnal sky, shine with incomparable radiance. The temple lays out a place where the elements come to be ranged alongside – and as they run together with – one another. It is a site of concurrence of the elements, of earth and sky, sea, and light. It brings into proximity what seem to be simply opposites: the massive solidity of stone and earth and the insubstantial spread of atmosphere and sky; the invisibility of light itself and the radiance of the marble illuminated by the light. As the very medium of irreducible elemental differences, it is itself utterly remote from ordinary things; it is something quite other, incomparably strange.

As the place where these elements come together in their very differences, the temple is not simply a temple of Poseidon but spreads around itself a precinct to which other gods too may draw near. For many centuries it was believed, on the basis of an erroneous report by Pausanias in the second century AD, that the temple at Sounion was dedicated to Athena. In fact, in antiquity there was a temple of Athena at Sounion; it stood some five hundred meters from the temple of Poseidon, on a lower hill, and is believed to have been the older of the two edifices. Today it is preserved only as a few blocks of marble outlining the rectangular shape of the temple. Yet not only Athena, patron goddess of the great maritime city, but also others of the immortals too were vitally linked to the sea and even, in some cases, as the Homeric passage shows regarding Apollo, to the sea gathered around the promontory at Sounion. Considering also, however, the complex identity of Apollo and especially his connection with light and the sun, this passage serves, in addition, to indicate that the site of the temple is distinctively related not only to the sea but to the elements at large.

Yet the great temple, erected on the highest plot of ground in the entire region, has a unique relation to Poseidon; and as a temple of Poseidon its character is preeminently determined by the sea, precisely as it is set high above on the rocky promontory. It is known that a sculpted figure of Poseidon once stood in the sekos, the middle chamber of the temple, though today no trace of it remains. For the ancients such sculpted figures were not mere representations of the gods, not mere copies or images showing how the gods looked, displaying their appearance, compensating thereby for the incapacity of humans for actually beholding the all too elusive gods. Rather, the sculpted figure served for enacting the placement of the god in the temple, his being offered the temple as a place where he was invited to enter and where, now and then, in his own elusive manner, he might reside. Just as the magnificent elevated site paid honor to the god, so the precipitous drop to the rocks and sea below displayed at this very site the destructiveness that Poseidon with his trident could unleash. Through the installing of the sculpted figure in the temple erected to house it, the god was invited to be present in the temple, was offered this presence in the hope, no doubt, that his graciousness rather than his destructiveness would prevail. In this sense the sculpted figure was nothing other than the god himself, his very way of being present in the temple.

But what, then, about the sea? How is it that the god who could come to be present in the temple remained, even when present there, the god of the sea? What does Poseidon – as the ancients experienced his presence – have to do with the sea?

It does not suffice to say that Poseidon inhabits the sea and reigns there like a king. For in this case there would be no need for mortals to build a habitation for the god; the temple and its sacred precinct would be entirely superfluous. Also, whereas for a king it is essential that he be beheld in all his glorious presence, Poseidon is, like all gods, perpetually elusive, hardly to be seen at all and often, if seen, seen only in some disguise or other. Nonetheless, mortals must somehow have caught sight of him even if only in a fleeting moment; otherwise they would erect no temple into which to invite the god and in which to celebrate his presence. Where, then, will the god have been caught sight of? Where will short-sighted mortals have caught a glimpse of Poseidon? Where will their fleeting glance have chanced upon the transient presence of the god? There is no other place than the sea. Poseidon is god of the sea, not because he would reign there as the godly analogue of a king, but rather because the sea is the place of his evanescent presence, the place where, on rare occasions, he lets humans catch sight of him. The sea is his element: not only *an* element, something elemental in distinction from mere things, but *his* element, the element in which he remains even as he comes to be present in the temple. Poseidon belongs to the depth of the sea, not just depth as opposed to surface, but depth in the sense of hidden retreat, of withdrawal into the utterly indefinite. There in his element the god remains unexposed to mortal eyes, withholds all offers of presence. And yet, from out of his element, from out of the depth of the sea, the god can unaccountably and fugitively appear. It is in such fleeting appearance that the Greeks experienced the most purely mythical.

Because the sea is his element, his appearance–fleeting though it be–can give one a glimpse of the true character of the sea. In the god, in the deeds that the poets revere as his, there is concentrated the graciousness and the destructiveness that belong to the thalassic element, that are bound together in its elemental character. While welcoming the god into the temple and celebrating his presence there may calm the disquieting element, these enactments never simply supersede the glimpse into the depth; neither do they silence the poets' songs of the god's deeds, but, on the contrary, they evoke, amplify them.

Though the temple is set overlooking the sea, its height above the sea is such that the god can enter it only by coming forth from the depth, yet without ever abandoning his element. Coming to presence in the darkened interior of the brilliantly illuminated temple, the god, glimpsed fleetingly, grants to mortals a momentary vision of other elements in their manifold concurrences with the sea.

Such glimpses, such visions, were granted–so they attest–to the Greeks.

And yet, now, one will say, the Greek gods – perhaps all gods – are dead. To whatever visions may have been granted to the ancients, we today, so it seems, can only remain blind.

And yet –

There, at that site, wonder may be evoked, wonder whether, in the presence of what remains of the temple, one can experience only the absence of the god, only the ruin of everything once sacred. Or whether, in envisioning the great temple that once stood overlooking the sea at Sounion, in engaging oneself imaginatively so as to let the temple take form from the traces that remain there, one can again experience the absolutely archaic. As the temple again takes shape – if now imaginatively – rising from the ruins at the very site where it once stood overlooking the sea and welcoming the brilliant Greek sunlight, can one sense the fleeting appearance of an origin of origins silently summoning from beyond what seems only closure?

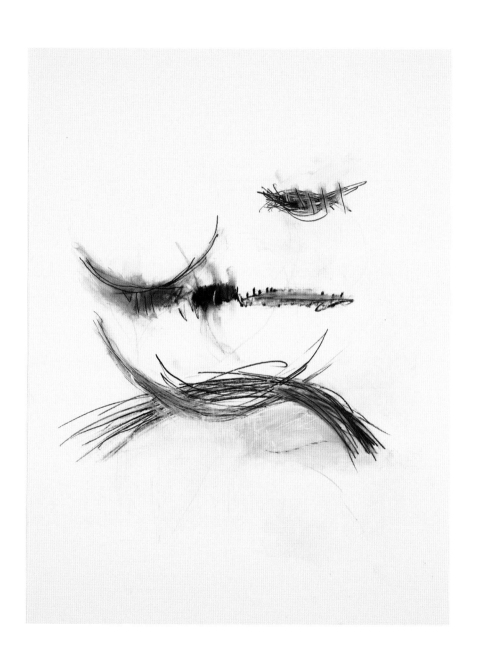

Poseidon
(Oil and pencil on
paper), 18×24 in.

5
Blues

Sounion
Attica

May

Standing atop the high promontory that juts out into the water, it is almost as if one were at sea completely out of sight of land. There at the edge of the precipice, little or nothing can be seen of the rocky earth; under the intense light of the cloudless day, virtually all that is visible is the sky and the sea. The Aegean stretches beyond to the horizon, which bounds the visible while remaining itself invisible; or rather, it appears only as the line that could be – but is not – drawn where the blue of the sea meets the lighter blue of the sky. It is a radiant world, prodigious in its transparency and simplicity, offering a consummate vision of the joining of air, sky, and sea. The vision is entirely cast in blue, with only minimal articulation. Nothing is to be seen that is not blue; nothing is to be seen but blue. While offering a vision of the concurrent elements, the vision is of blue as such, of blueness itself.

Yet it will be said that there can be no vision of sheer blue, of blue as such, that blueness itself can never be manifest to our visual sense. It will be said that what can be seen is never simply blue and nothing else, that in our experience we never catch sight of a blue that is nothing other than blue, of a blue that is only blue, only itself. The belief–an age-old belief–is that such self-same, self-enfolded beings can only be said, not seen. When we speak of blueness itself or even when we merely think of it without actually voicing the words that designate it, it is then somehow present to us, as if evoked by our words or thoughts. And yet, its presence is quite unlike that of what we see around us, of the bluebird we see winging its way through the air to light on a limb of a nearby tree and sing its heart out. Blueness itself displays neither movement nor sonority. Its presence–if it can indeed be present in a sense that does not violate the sense of the word–is of an entirely different kind, an invisible presence that is, at once, both distant, in its invisibility, and near, in its responsiveness to our evocation of it in speech or thought. Nothing is more enigmatic: as color it is a paragon of visibility, and yet it is wholly invisible.

Could this invisible blueness ever be evoked without any reference to the blue that we actually see around us? If it is wholly invisible, how could there ever arise any assurance that it pertains to the radiant blue that we behold around us? In some manner or other, this strange, invisible presence must be deflected back toward the visibility that would govern its very bearing; it must somehow be bent back in the direction of the blue of sea, of sky, of things, the very sense of which it is alleged to express.

Is it not, then, there amidst the visible that blue is preeminently to be found? Is it not indeed starting from the visible that we can come to speak of what is blue and thus to evoke this strange invisible double of what is preeminently visible, this unseen spectre of the very tissue of visibility? Though the word may regulate the range of what is called blue, what gives sense (in every sense) to the word is preeminently the vision of the blue that surrounds us. Yet because the word must be given its sense, what it designates is set apart from what one would like to call – but cannot simply call – blueness itself. Because it receives its sense rather than bearing it in itself, what it signifies must be differentiated from the blue that shines within a visible spectacle. The blue that is said never simply coincides with the blue that is seen.

Blue is to be seen, perhaps most conspicuously, among things. In nature there are birds and flowers that are blue and through human fabrication a host of other things. If in observing such things we focus on the mere fact that they are blue, then we will implicitly have broached a difference between the thing itself and the blue that belongs to it. Our language has long since been shaped to accommodate and remark this difference both by assuming its very form and by expressing it as the inherence of a property or quality in a thing. And yet, precisely because blueness merely inheres in them, the things seen around us do not offer a vision of blueness itself. For, as property of a thing, it is as if this quality were owned by the thing, as if it were bonded property. Blueness proves to be tightly bound to the thing, not in the manner of two units forming a dyad but rather in that of an interlacement so intricate that there is no point where the difference can actually be marked.

Neither the thing nor its blueness can as such be beheld. The thing can appear only through its blueness and whatever other properties it possesses. We never see a thing itself entirely stripped of its properties, reduced to complete indigence; neither is it even certain whether there *is* a thing as such completely apart from its properties. And, while the thing appears only through such properties as its blueness, this blueness appears, not as such, not simply as itself, but as the blueness of the thing to which it belongs. As soon as we undertake to detach blue from the thing, to conceive it apart, we have begun to transfer its sense to something less seen than thought.

Yet there is a way to detach color from things without withdrawing it from sight. In painting, it can be presented as both detached from things and yet still to an extent linked to them: as detached it ceases to be merely the color of things, becomes free color, color itself, and yet, as still linked to things and as fully sensuously present, it remains entirely visible, forgoes the shift toward mere intelligibility. In certain of Kandinsky's *Compositions,* for instance, color expands beyond or even leaps over the boundaries of the things to which it nonetheless does not entirely cease to belong. In this way color is freed from enclosure within things and given a life outside where it can appear as what it is. Perhaps nothing is more requisite for painting than the capacity for such liberating transposition, especially if, adapting Klee's celebrated dictum, it is color and not the representation of colored things that makes a painter a painter.

The question is whether such free color as that to which painting attests is to be found in nature. Where, if not amidst things, is it to be sought?

It suffices to look out again across the Aegean, training our eyes on this open expanse of sea and sky, on what is offered to vision there. It is essential to engage our vision silently, even as we observe and say that what is seen is nothing but blue, nothing but various shades of blue. The blue of the sky is no property, does not belong to anything, but radiates freely before our vision. The sky is not a thing in which the quality blue inheres. It is not a thing at all, and we only violate its way of appearing if we insist on applying to it the ancient schema of things having properties. The brilliant diurnal sky cannot even properly be said *to be blue,* for it is nothing else – shines forth as nothing else – than blueness, a distinctive blueness indeed, a uranic blueness, but not the blueness of something that *is* blue. Indeed, from a panoptic or extraterrestrial point of view, the sky *is not* at all; there is no such thing as the sky.

It is not so different with the blue of the sea. To be sure, its textures are more varied and complex: there is differentiation between surface and depth; there is the motion of the waves; and there are on its surface the lighter traces that pattern the directions of the wind. But its relatively boundless, nonperspectival look shows that it is an element and not a thing possessing properties. Its legendary wine-dark color is not simply bound to it but ranges freely throughout it.

In a certain way the free-ranging blue of sky and sea displays an affinity with the invisible blue evoked in speech. For in both instances blueness itself is detached from things, freed from incorporation within things. But in another way these blues could hardly be more different. The blue of sky and sea shines forth directly to our vision with a brilliance that the mere blue of things can never match. How pale, then, how ghostlike the blue that is merely said must seem when confronted with the radiant, free blueness of sky and sea!

If we would know what blue is, then it behooves us to look out across the sea, out to the horizon where it meets the sky, and to train our sense to the recessive presence by which the blue beheld there utterly escapes what can be said of blue, indeed even in the word itself. Such training requires, above all, a discipline of silence.

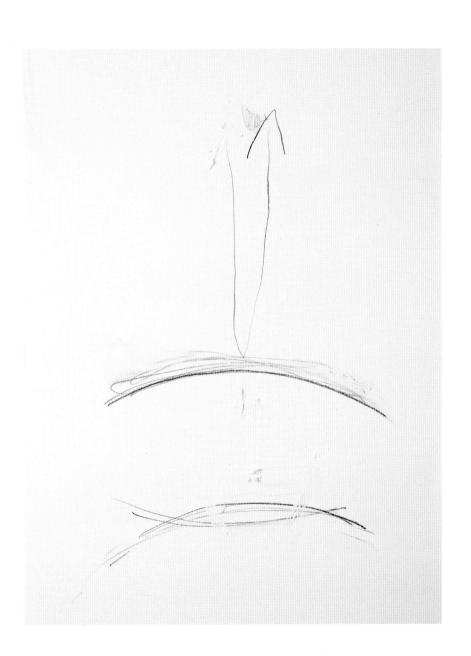

Summer I
(Oil and pencil on
paper), 12×18 in.

Summer II
(Oil and pencil on
paper), 18×24 in.

Summer III
(Oil and pencil on
paper), 18×24 in.

6
City of Lights

Paris

May

These are days when the sky is pure light spreading its gift across the expanse of the city, casting its luminous splendor on the boulevards and the monuments, the gardens and the palaces. On such days the light shines with such intensity that it actually produces the opposite of its usual effect, assuming the guise of a gift that in being given also takes back a certain measure of what it bestows. Instead of making things visible, it renders them virtually invisible; they come to be wrapped in light, enshrouded by it, concealed. In the very midst of things there appear blank spaces in which only the resplendent sunlight is to be seen, ellipses of visibility that are neither simply visible nor simply invisible. These intervals of excessive luminosity repel sustained vision; they yield only to the momentary glance. The light that conceals, that renders things invisible rather than making them visible, proves so elusive that it virtually conceals itself. Ever so fleeting, this luminous concealment borders on utter self-concealment.

Walking along the quai next to the Seine, one hardly sees the water, but only the sparkling reflections of sunlight on its surface. The pattern of the reflections constantly dissolves and again takes shape as the gentle waves spread across the river. Occasionally the pattern is disturbed by a boat crowded with squinting sightseers as it makes its way toward Pont Neuf. One wonders what they will have seen under this blinding sunlight; indeed one wonders what they would have seen otherwise, even in this city that offers so much to see to those who have eyes to see it. For seeing is not merely perceiving in the sense of having a series of impressions register on one's visual endowment. Rather, what is to be seen must be taken up in its visible display in such a way that its contours of shading, color, and delineation come to be retraced. On the other hand, seeing is not mere recognition; it is not merely tagging the visible thing as something familiar, as a mere instance of something known beforehand with a knowledge to which the sight of this singular instance has little or nothing to contribute. Rather, genuine seeing requires a certain abstention from thoughts, opinions, preconceptions; it requires a sustained refusal to let the transition from sense to signification come into play, a refusal to think abstractly in the manifest presence of the visible site, a refusal of the move on past it that, instead of remaining intent on the visible, would proceed to say what it is. Thus, seeing demands also that speech be impeded, that one remain reticent, even silent, so that both the visible site and all that contributes to its peculiar visibility can become apparent in their full—yet also always elusive—manifestness.

The trees along both banks reflect the splendor of the day. Their leaves not only glisten in the blazing light but also sway to and fro in the gentle breeze like silent bells that would ring out a celebration of the day. They also assume the role of tiny, rotating mirrors that lend their assistance to the light by casting it in all directions.

If, turning away from the river, one approaches the easternmost entrance to the vast edifice, the great museum appears more than ever to resemble a Greek temple gleaming under the brilliant sunlight. Its façade is almost entirely illuminated; there is little more than a hint of shadows even in the spaces behind the great Corinthian columns. The friezes are visible in every detail as if they had been transported directly from the Parthenon itself, translating their tales of gods and heroes from the ancient to the modern city.

The large courtyard that leads toward the actual entrance to the museum is flooded with light, as if it were a huge receptacle designed to receive and hold the radiance of the day. Just beyond is the pyramid, which shelters the entrance and which is virtually the opposite of the courtyard leading to it: not only does it beckon upward to the diurnal light, but also, because of its transparency, it lets the light freely pass through. The pyramid is flanked by fountains that shoot the water upward with such force that under the intense sunlight its appearance is more like that of light itself than of water, as if in its ascent the water were transmuted into light.

Inside the museum, too, there is light, and not just that produced by artificial lighting or let in through windows or skylights. In entering the museum, one exchanges the intense sunlight for the light that shines from within paintings. It is not merely a case of works in which light would be a theme depicted in the way that a person or a landscape might be depicted. Rather, it is a matter of paintings that excel in realizing the capacity of art to let light be seen *as* light, to bring to appearance that by which we see things but which for the most part, in seeing things, we hardly see at all. In this regard what counts is the way in which painting makes visible the virtually invisible source or means of visibility.

There is light and visibility in various registers. Among these is the vision opened up by the poet as well as the light of poetic inspiration that makes such vision possible. It is in this register that light is painted in Poussin's *The Inspiration of the Poet*. In this painting the light of inspiration, along with its transmission, is portrayed precisely through the depiction of natural light, which shines on the face of inspiring Apollo as, backed by similarly illuminated Calliope (muse of epic poetry), he dictates to the poet (often identified as Virgil). There is light also on Apollo's right arm as he points to the poet's manuscript, that is, as he effects the translation of the vision inspired into the poetic word. The light illuminating his leg may offer a subtle reminder that poetic inspiration is something that simply comes upon the scene, not something that can be cultivated or learned. The face of the poet himself is much less illuminated, as if to suggest that he, receiving the gift of inspiration, is more scribe than visionary.

In La Tour's *Magdalen by a Night-Light* the subject is seated next to a table on which is burning a candle, which casts its light on her face and upper body. Her illuminated face is seen in profile as she stares at the flame, not as though observing it but rather with the look of someone sunk into deep meditation. On the table are two large, closed books and in front of them a wooden crucifix and a rope with which to chastise herself. On her lap is a skull on which her right hand is placed. The picture thus presents her as suspended between, on the one side, the light of the candle, along with tokens of the illumination engendered by learning, faith, and self-discipline, and, on the other side, the inevitability of death, the fate of mortality. As, in her meditation, she looks to the light yet also touches the emblem of death, she senses, no doubt, that these are the extremes between which the lives of humans are stretched. For the absolute other of the light is not simply the dark; as shadow, dark always accompanies and complements light, and as night, it always portends the light of day. The absolute other of light is, rather, death; and, as Homer declared, to live is to behold the light of the sun.

Vermeer's *The Astronomer* presents the light born of the new scientific knowledge and the enlightenment engendered by the opening of new horizons through exploration and discovery and through new, more powerful means of observation such as the telescope. Now the light comes from without, shining through the window and illuminating the face of the astronomer. It also illuminates the top of the table at which he is seated and, in particular, the globe, which he turns as if enacting a journey to some faraway, unexplored corner of the world. In addition to the books atop the adjacent chest and the scientific chart attached to it, there is an open book lying on the table before the astronomer. The book, which has been identified as Metius' *On the Observation of Stars,* is brightly lit by the light streaming in through the window. It is the open book of the new science and of the expanding vision of the world and of the cosmos.

If one has experienced the manifold presences in which this city both displays and harbors such a wealth of light in all these registers, then one will perhaps be tempted to say again, as was said by a famous visitor to Paris nearly two centuries ago, that it is the capital of the civilized world. For Hegel, like the ancients, never ceased to affirm that it is in turning to the light, in engaging the ascendancy that advances toward the light, that human excellence is furthered, that, in his idiom, the advent of spirit, its return to itself, is achieved. And, at the very least, the civilized is set apart from the barbarian by its promotion of such excellence, by its aiding in the advent of spirit.

Temple I
(Oil and pencil on
paper), 18×24 in.

Temple II
(Oil and pencil on
paper), 18×24 in.

7
Time's Shadows

Saint-Hippolyte
Alsace

June

Around the time of the summer solstice the sunlight can become
almost unbearable both in its intensity and in its duration. Yet it was
a fitting time to chance upon a remarkable instrument by which, in a
former time, sunlight provided the measure of time. I found it on the
side of an old house in the nearby village of Bergheim. Set between two
second-story windows above a small shop, the astronomical sundial
consists of a painted square some two meters wide from which extend
three metal rods. On the white background there is superimposed, near
the top, an image of the sun; it is represented as a radiant face. Above
the sun face there are two inscriptions. The first reads: "Sicut umbra
fugit vita" (Life is fleeting just like a shadow), while the other, just
below the first, indicates that the sundial was made in 1711. From the
face of the sun, arrows radiate out – to the side and downward – to two
three-sided bands running along the sides and the bottom of the square;

on the bands are inscribed the hours of sunrise and sunset, the signs of the zodiac, and the months of the year. Along both sides of the arrow that points directly downward, the hours of the day are indicated. At the center of the square, directly below the face of the sun, two of the metal rods extend at an angle from two points on the surface, meeting so as to form with the surface an equilateral triangle. From the point where these two rods meet, a third, longer rod extends upward to the face of the sun. It is from the shadow that the three connected rods cast across the surface of the sundial that the various determinations of time can be read off, most directly the time of year (the month) and the time of day (the hour). It is the shadow that gives the measure of time; and it can hardly have been simply by chance that the inscribed word that is placed at the very top of the sundial directly above the face of the sun is *umbra*.

When I first came across the sundial in midafternoon, a few clouds had gathered, blocking the direct sunlight so that no shadow was to be seen on the sundial. Without seeing the time-measuring shadow, it was difficult to discern just how the instrument performs its function. But once the sun reappeared, the shadow was cast, and the functioning of the sundial was evident. There appeared two long triangles, one inscribed in the other and sharing up to a point its (unmarked) base. The longer triangle extended down well below the sundial onto the bare side of the house, while the other came just about to the bottom of the painted surface. The one side of the longer triangle that it shared to an extent with the other triangle formed the indicative part of the shadow: it crossed the central, downward-pointing arrow at precisely the point designating—correctly—that it was 4:00 PM in the month of June.

Through its connection with the sunlight, such an instrument measures time concretely, in contrast to the abstract measure provided by mechanical clocks. For the means on which it depends, namely, sunlight and its effect, is none other than that by which time – its hours and seasons – is naturally determined.

The time that is determined in this way is that of nature, or rather, of the space encompassed by the natural elements, preeminently by earth and sky. It is the time that holds sway in this natural abode of humans and of the other living things known to us, all of which are subject to the comings and goings of sunlight and all that accompanies the alternation of day and night and the course of the seasons. We can of course abstract from this naturally measured time, measuring it instead by reference to other regularly recurring phenomena such as the swinging of a pendulum or the frequency of a certain radiation; yet such measures typically retain some reference back to the natural measurement. It is indicative of our bond to the natural measure of time that even where the measure is extended completely beyond our natural abode and applied to cosmic phenomena such as stars and galaxies, the measuring units are still derived from the natural measure of time. Hence, the course of a star's evolution is determined in terms of years, even though it may be situated at an enormous distance from the earth, by which, in its relation to our sun, the year is determined; and the distance between cosmic phenomena is calculated in light-years.

.   .   .   .

Within the enchorial domain in which we pass our lives, nothing is more concretely and directly indicative of time than light and its effects. The intensity and directness of the sunlight mark the course of the day and of the year. Shadows can be equally indicative, not only on a sundial but also as, for instance, they lengthen in late afternoon, announcing the advance toward evening. Variations in the color of sunlight also measure the course of the day, from the brilliant colors of dawn and dusk to the sheer transparency of the midday light.

In very northern regions the time around the summer solstice is marked by the overabundance of sunlight, by the long duration of daylight, which reduces the night to no more than a few hours, and still farther north banishes it entirely. This time is marked also by an alteration in the exchange between daylight and darkness. No longer is sunset followed almost immediately by nightfall; rather, it is as if the day lingers in an extended twilight, deferring nightfall far into the nighttime hours. Twilight goes on and on, as if time itself were slowed by the persistence of the light and everything transposed into a state of suspension. Even the pace of human activity is slowed, and we are tempted to linger in this time that is neither simply day nor simply night. It is as if the day were stretched into the night, as if they came to overlap in a time-span identifiable as neither, having a character all its own.

Though even here in Alsace summer days are long, the cool nights bring respite from the abundance of sunlight. Both are essential to another temporality that in this location can hardly be overlooked. From the wine village of Saint-Hippolyte there stretches out onto the Rhine plain an expanse of vineyards that, in the other direction, continues up the slopes of the Vosges Mountains. In this region time is inseparable from the progression by which the bare vines again come to life and the wine-grapes appear, mature, and at the appropriate time are ready for harvest. At each stage the sunlight–its directness, intensity, and duration–is instrumental to such an extent that its variation in the course of the season marks the various stages of growth and production. In the wine itself there will remain a trace of the sunlight.

.   .   .

On the day after the solstice, a huge cloud coming from the west brought welcome relief from the sunlight. As the cloud moved in, it grew ever darker, and soon it had stretched across almost the entire sky. The cool air that it brought had the feel of a thunderstorm, a feel irreducible to mere feeling or smell or any other of the conventional rubrics by which we try, without much success, to capture our experiences of elemental nature. The cloud continued to expand toward the eastern horizon where the mountains of the Black Forest on the other side of the Rhine plain could still, for a while, be seen in silhouette. Before it quite reached the horizon, it abruptly halted its expansion, leaving exposed only the band of light that stretched around the eastern horizon. Then for a time the black canopy hovered like an ominous shadow or a giant umbrella over the broad landscape. It was as if, with its expansion across the sky, this gigantic shade marked the time of the storm. For as soon as the umbrella had opened, leaving only the band of brightness around the horizon, the storm immediately commenced: driving rain, blown in all directions by the strong winds; disheveled trees adding their voice to the sound of the pounding rain; lightning with thunder echoing again and again in the mountains at my back; all animate creatures gone, having taken shelter from the elements. Once the storm had fully commenced, the black canopy again began to expand and soon obscured entirely the eastern horizon. It was then fully the time of the storm. It would extend into the evening hours, the fury of the storm gradually abating, until finally nightfall came to seal the darkness.

8
The Light
Spread
of Time

Münstertal
Baden

June

The day is exquisite as it spreads its light over the entire valley. The scattered clouds are as brilliantly white as the sky is intensely blue. From this brilliance and intensity along with the sharpness with which the clouds are outlined against the sky, it can be seen that the air, at this moment, is exceptionally transparent, utterly diaphanous. The phenomenon is remarkable: the transparent air can, in this sense, be seen – directly, not by way of inference – even though it is not itself seen, not seen as such. It appears precisely in remaining the invisible, perfect medium of another appearing. It comes to light, not by reflecting light, as do things, but by giving free passage to light. Visibility, it appears, is not limited to visible things but can be bestowed on something invisible in and of itself, indeed in such a way that precisely its invisibility is what comes to light.

The clouds drift slowly along, their shapes gradually transforming as they become more airy and expansive or contract into denser forms, also as they extend wispy appendages toward other forms, some slowly merging, some separating into new shapes, in a play of resolution and dissolution that contests the very category of individuality. Nothing illustrates more concretely and immaculately the sense of *drift* than this light, airy show of forms. The play requires for its stage only the absolutely immobile diurnal sky. Yet the uniformity of the sky prevents it from providing a measure for the movement; it merely forms the expanse on which the drifting clouds can be observed in relation to each other.

Most of the clouds are gathered just above the ridge that bounds the valley on the north side. A pine forest stretches up the mountainside to the ridge; moreover, many of the trees on the upper slope are of such height that their tops extend above the ridge itself. Thus the contour that marks the upper bound of the mountainside is provided, in effect, with a series of vertical measuring rods in relation to which a trained eye can readily gauge the drift of the clouds. It is as if calibration had been inscribed by nature in this region where the dense forest and rocky mountainside give way to light, to open air, and to sky.

Time is everywhere. Its ubiquity is not only like that of the day, spread evenly over everything; the spread is also such that time is lightly, unobtrusively marked, that it leaves its trace, amidst all things as well as in regions defined not primarily by things but by the elements, indeed most conspicuously in these regions. It is marked in the drift of the light clouds along the ridge; and the natural measure provided by the protruding treetops is, in effect, to the trained eye, a kind of natural clock. The forest, too, bears its trace of time: set against the heavier, darker growth that has endured the winter, the abundance of fresh, light green with which the pines are now decorated bespeaks the advent of early summer. The intensely blue, cloudless sky overhead offers a visible promise of several hours of sunshine to come. Yet in the air there is a hint – ever so slight – of a change that late afternoon may bring, a hint that is conveyed – ever so slightly – to our sensing. It would be difficult to say how it is conveyed: perhaps by the slightest of scents, by a scent so light and so momentary that one would have no sense of its origin; perhaps by the delicate feel of slightly cooler, slightly moist air on the skin – in any case by sensings that cannot be readily accommodated to the conventional concepts of the five senses. For this reason, the doubly vague concept of feeling is readily introduced to describe such sensing. Yet to those fully acclimated to this region, it is anything but vague; rather, it portends – as definitely as portentions allow – a thunderstorm to come. Animals often feel such portentions much more intensely than do humans and much farther in advance of the occasion portended. When our weaker premonition hardly senses at all what is to come, the behavior even of a domesticated animal – the nervous pacing of a dog, for instance – may show that in this connection the animal's sense of the future extends – like certain other animal senses – well beyond the human's. For itinerant humans it may be only when the dark, threatening clouds begin to form over the mountains to the east of the valley that a sense of the coming storm is awakened. It is they who are much more confined within the present moment than the animals. To the extent that they are out of touch, in every sense, with the elements, they lose also a certain natural perceptiveness to the spread of time. They fail to catch even a glimpse of how time is spread amidst the elements, of how the early morning chill is still present (as past) in the

cool breeze of midday, of how the light gusts in midafternoon portend
the strong wind that toward nightfall will bring cold air from the north.
Unless they are attentive to the course of the natural elements, they
may overlook the tiny bud that has just begun to swell in early spring;
and they may miss the inconspicuous appearance of the traces of color
that first announce the advent of fall.

It is in such ways, then, that sky, forest, air, and clouds convey
the arrival of the season, the promise held in the present, and the
portentions of what is to come. Thus does time inscribe its traces
in all these places. There, for those who are perceptive, it is to be
seen – indeed not only seen but also sensed in other ways, as when an
animal catches a scent that warns of a still unseen danger to come; or
as when, in late winter, the warmth of the returning sunshine evokes
spontaneous memories of summers past and joyful expectations of the
one to come. The spread of time is also to be heard, as when, in the not
too distant high mountains, a call returns as an echo so as to sound
the measure of its doubled passage; or as when, in a thunderstorm, the
rolling of thunder sounds its measure in accord with the contours of the
valley.

The sounding of time lends itself to enhancement by means of
human fabrications. The tolling of the church bells both declares, in
their sounding, the time of day and spreads this measure of time across
the entire valley to even the most remote farmhouse, making it audible
to all. The strokes communicate intimately with our most concrete
sense of time. They indicate by way of number what part of the day has
passed and what part has still to come before sunset arrives to turn
day into night. Thus the sounding of the bells brings number, hence

measure, to bear on our otherwise inarticulate sense of passingness. Little is altered if the sounding is shifted to the city, only that the sounding is situated in a more abstract setting, the significance of its measure now being determined in reference, not to the natural limits of the day, but to humanly instituted articulations. But even then, when night can be turned into day, it is the same spread of time that persists.

The bells of the village church may also sound the time of celebration, a time set apart from the everyday because it either is or memorializes an event of exceptional significance. The bells may also announce the time of a death. Their somber tolling tells that someone in the valley has come to the time that bounds and binds human existence. In a small village most will know who it is that has died, and there remains an openness of death in contrast to the often prevailing tendency to render it inaudible and invisible. In hearing the tolling of death, we are most concretely and profoundly reminded that life is a gift bestowed by time, that its span is a spread of time.

Whereas clocks are more punctual and, especially in the case of digitals, show a point of time at precisely that time, bells have a different kind of relation to the time they announce. Though the first stroke of the bells is set to occur at the very time to be announced, it is at this point undetermined – at any rate, unknown to the auditor – how many strokes will follow and hence what the time actually is that is being announced. Yet when the final stroke is sounded – or rather, when, after the sounding of the final stroke, the ensuing silence reveals that it was the final stroke – and it is then known what the time is that has been announced, it is no longer that time at all but is already later. Thus, when the first stroke sounds, the time is not yet announced; but after the final sounding has passed, the time is no longer that which will have been announced, but rather time will then already have spread into a further span yet to be measured and announced.

In sounding the measure of time, the bells spread time beyond the point, attesting thereby to the elusive passingness of time. Because of its light passage, because it passes as imperceptibly as light traverses a clear, open space, time too has its space; or rather, it opens a space through which it can spread, leaving or prompting here and there, in the places where we pass our lives, traces of its passage.

9
Heights

Tristachersee
Osttirol

July

Favor is always granted to the upward look. Vision is invariably drawn to the heights, as if by nature, as if orientation to the upward way were indigenous to human nature, inscribed there by nature itself. Not even the most extreme obsession with things close at hand or with their bearing on us can render us entirely insensitive to the force of attraction to the heights. This force not only draws vision upward but also, as the heights open up, recoils earthward, comes over us, eliciting affective simulation of the sublime ascent that vision will already have traced. Transposed ecstatically to the soaring heights, we take joy in being released, even if only imaginatively, from the bonds that bind us to the earth. The limits of earthbound existence fade before the age-old phantasy of flight.

There is music that not only awakens this joy of ascent but also lets it resound, translating both vision and affection into measured tones. As always in art, this redoubling makes manifest what otherwise would merely be enacted, would simply be undergone. The tones transgress the conventional boundaries between the senses; they evoke a vision of the heights and a sense, neither simply visual nor simply aural, of the site of the ascent. As the music soars and then in a moment of exhalation prepares to soar still higher, it replicates artistically the attraction to the heights and the imaginative, affective engagement in the ascent.

There are places, uncommon places, where the attraction of the heights is visibly displayed in an exemplary manner–as at this unique site in the Dolomites where the sheer vertical face of a mountain forms the backdrop of a shallow but heavily forested area, which is bordered frontally by an Alpine lake. The forested area is so thickly packed with various species of evergreens that almost no light penetrates their canopy to the ground below. Because of their bare, but straight, slender trunks and because of the way their upper branches point, like arrows, upward to the heights, the trees display an extreme verticality. Seen from the other side of the lake, they chart a visual course that leads on up toward the cliff that appears to form the summit of the mountain. It is a natural course, not only charted by nature but also laid out as if it were addressed to our vision, as if it were designed to entice vision to take it up.

Yet how is it that even where this course is not so compellingly charted by nature itself our vision strives upward and evokes in us a longing for elevation? What is it about the heights that exercises such attraction? How is it that, even when an upward way is not visibly manifest, we project it in imagination, in speech, or in thought? How is it that, in the guise of image, sign, or idea, the heights represent primacy of rank, of value, or even of being? Does nature itself give force to such representation?

In any case, at this Alpine site the upward way is visibly manifest: it leads beyond the forest to the vertical face of the mountain and onward, upward, toward the summit. On the face of the mountain there are several areas where vertical striations appear to mark and enhance the sheer verticality of the mountain. Along what appears to be the summit, there is a line of trees that caps the vertical face. Silhouetted against the sky, marking the pinnacle of ascent while also gesturing toward the immeasurable height of the heaven, this scene of seemingly limitless elevation readily evokes phantasies of a beyond, phantasies that have never ceased to shape the aspirations and hopes that we humans share.

It is almost impossible – so it is said – to reach the summit, and in any case it is extremely dangerous to try; it is as if the mountain withheld itself from human intrusion. Yet farther down, around its base, there are abundant signs of human intervention, including indeed our very presence. Yet if one turns aside and casts one's gaze along the length of the lake and on beyond, a towering range of mountains is to be seen in the distance; there no signs of human habitation or intervention are, from this distance, visible. The upper reaches of the mountains, almost devoid of trees, have the look of sheer stone. Most remarkable are the voluminous cumulus clouds that float just above the mountaintops, consorting with them so as to let earth and sky appear in utter proximity while maintaining their elemental difference. The appearance is of bright, weightless, drifting clouds as they momentarily touch the dark, massive, upward-thrusting stone.

Yet it is otherwise with the lake: it appears to lack entirely the verticality that marks the rest of the scene. Even when a gentle wind produces a pattern of ripples or a water fowl leaves a tiny wake spreading across the surface, the directionality of the lake itself is entirely horizontal, entirely lacking in height. Nonetheless, by virtue of its capacity to mirror the surroundings, the water lets verticality appear, despite remaining alien to it as such. In its vivid, shimmering reflection of the forest that surrounds it, the lake offers an image of height, and the calmer it becomes, the more distinct are the contours of the images.

There are other kinds of reflections that by their very indistinctness are all the more remarkable. On a calm day they can be seen around midmorning, provided the sun casts a light sheen on the surface of the lake, illuminating the texture formed by the slight ripples that spread across it. Along the bank there is a sprawling evergreen with branches, mostly bare, reaching down almost to the water. On the few branches that are filled out with needles, the pattern of the ripples is reflected; it is clearly identifiable on the simulation of surface that the filled-out branches provide. On the other hand, what is utterly remarkable—indeed astonishing when first seen—are the traces of the light on the bare branches. What is produced is not a reflection at all in any usual sense; there is no image of the water's surface, nothing that doubles the appearance of the surface. Rather, what one sees are spots of light running up some branches and down others, up toward the tree trunk where, once they reach the larger branches, they disappear, down toward the water as if rejoining the rippling surface by which they were cast. Though cast from that surface as it reflects the sunlight, these sunspots running up and down the branches bear not the slightest resemblance to the water's surface. These reflections that reflect nothing have, instead, the look of free parcels of light wandering along the branches as they please. And yet, they are reflections: for as soon as the sun moves behind the clouds, the entire spectacle of these little traces of light vanishes entirely.

The surface of the lake provides a mirror for all manner of reflections, reflections not only of or onto the surrounding forest but also of the configuration of clouds. Indeed, with the approach of night, a remarkable, almost paradoxical kind of reflection of the clouds makes its appearance. In the diminished light of dusk, the images cast by the clouds become more intense; their lines, their contours, and even their voluminosity come to be more vividly reflected on the surface of the lake. Finally, when the darkness has almost descended on the entire scene, the images of the intensely white cumulus clouds appear with such density and such accentuated contours that they begin to look more like a magical, moon-lit snowfield than like mere reflections of airy shapes. Hence the paradoxical character of the appearance: the less light there is, the more intensely the clouds are mirrored by the surface of the water, until finally, when the light has almost entirely withdrawn, the very appearance of the image, its look, is thoroughly transformed.

In the images that the clouds cast on the surface of the lake, the two elements, the aerial and the thalassic, coalesce. Moreover, the airy forms, giving texture to the sky, draw it, too, into the reflections, so as to occasion at the surface of the water a concurrence of virtually all the elements. Precisely because it occurs purely by way of reflection, such concurrence can serve, in turn, to focus attention on the most elemental articulations, those by which the regions of the various elements are set apart, air from sea, earth from sky.

It is not only within nature that the heights exercise their attraction and declare their preeminence. Even with what lies at the limit of nature, whatever is uppermost proclaims thereby its preeminence. The Greek mythos is exemplary: though it declares that over each of the three regions into which all things are divided a god is assigned to rule, Hades over the homonymous underworld, Poseidon over the sea, and Zeus over the heaven, it declares, too, unconditionally, that Zeus, ruler over the uppermost region, is the god who is supreme.

The preeminence of the heights is attested not only in nature and myth but also in art, most manifestly at those points where art touches on the presence and absence of the divine. The verticality of a Gothic cathedral makes visibly manifest that which is of such preeminence that it cannot become simply visible as such but can only be shown by way of the extreme verticality of the architectural form. Because the gods withdraw to the heights, human aspirations, if excessive, become perilous; and stories abound of those whose heedless ventures into the heaven resulted in their ruin.

In antiquity the preeminence of the heights and the attractive force it exercises upon humans were represented in figural guise and in narratives of ascent. These representations were, in turn, detached from their original site and themselves submitted to the very elevation they represented. Thus they came to represent the preeminence and attractive force of an origin beyond what was, to sense, the manifest origin of the light that lets all things become visible. This still more preeminent origin, itself withdrawn from sense, could only be itself represented by construing the visible origin, the source of visibility, as an image of it. The look of the sun high in the heaven casting light upon the scene of all other things becomes the image from which the ascent to the truly preeminent is to commence and by which, on its course, it would continue to be sustained. Without this sustenance human aspiration would be left wandering in a void without the slightest sense of direction.

In all these attestations and transpositions of height, what remains manifestly preeminent is the sky and the gift of light that it envelops and bestows on all things. Its height is, in a sense, absolute: not only is its height such that it cannot be reached, but, still further, it is entirely inconceivable what it would mean to reach or not to reach the sky. Only the utmost fancy could picture our coming to touch it. To be sure, there are many things in nature that convey a sense of height and of the enhancement of vision that is bestowed by height. The sheer vertical face of the mountain draws vision upward and prompts us to imagine the breadth that vision would enjoy from there on high. The elements, too, that come from above, the rain, hail, snow, lightning, and thunder, contribute to the sense of the uranic source. Yet the ultimate measure of height, itself beyond measure, is the sky itself enveloping and bestowing light. What attests most manifestly to the preeminence of height is the light of the sky.

Alturas (Heights)
(Oil and pencil on
paper), 18×24 in.

10
Summer
Snow

Seefeld
Tirol

July

Even though it is midsummer, almost a month after the solstice, yesterday brought a fairly heavy snowfall in the mountains. As we drove up
through the pass, the temperature plummeted, and the heavy rain and
thick fog deprived all but the immediate surroundings of its visibility.
There could be little doubt but that higher up, around the soaring
peaks, snow was falling. Yet, as night came on to enshroud everything,
enclosing even the fog and clouds in darkness, not even the slightest
glimpse of the raging elements above was possible. We would have to
wait until morning.

Morning brought the tranquility that follows the storm. Now
nature's assault has given way to the assurance offered by the few
cumulus clouds that drift across the otherwise clear sky. On the
mountain peaks the snow glistens in the intense light of the summer
sun. Its pure whiteness, quite different from the dull gray of glacial ice,

bespeaks that it is light and fleeting. Clearly it will last only for a short time. By evening it will almost be gone. By tomorrow hardly a trace will remain.

Both in color and in its visible texture the glistening snow contrasts with the bare rock that protrudes here and there, especially where the mountainside is at its steepest. There are also places where the snow reaches down past the tree line. Within these areas extending down toward the forest, the exchange between ice and stone that prevails on the peaks gives way to an inverted and distorted semblance of growth, as if the dark evergreens grew up out of the purely white ground, as if growth were from light to dark rather than from the dark earth into the light.

Especially under such rare conditions, the Alpine peaks provide, more than ever, a place where the elements are gathered, a place for this gathering. As sheer stone the earth thrusts upward, its verticality reversing what seems the natural tendency and place of this element. The snow gathered on the peaks is equally out of place at this time of year when all but the most tenacious glacial ice should have undergone its natural transformation and streamed down into the valley below to water all that humans have planted and tended there. The contour of this gathering of stone and ice, of earth and water, appears sharply against the sky, which is given texture and pattern by the voluminous clouds. The puffy white clouds appear darker than usual by contrast with the snow. And yet, when the sun breaks through the clouds, the snow on the peaks shines so intensely that it is as if it were a mirror reflecting the surrounding clouds with such brilliance that the purest white is restored – or even first granted – to them. Yet it is the mountain peaks that provide the fulcrum, the focal point, or rather the visible expanse where the elements come together. In their majestic ascendancy and radiant shining, they provide a place where earth and water, sky and the upper air are gathered, a place where they concur in an elemental proximity. Here there is made visible in their lines of articulation the four presences that the Greeks took to be the roots or elements of all things; or at least there is made visible something like what the Greeks named in words that remain virtually untranslatable and that most certainly are not conveyed by the usual names that we give to the elements. For this reason it is imperative that we not be captivated by our own form of speech but endeavor instead to experience anew and to say anew elemental nature as nature itself brings it into view or sets before us the script in which the elemental is encoded.

In the shining of the snow atop the mountains, the light, which makes all things visible, is itself granted a distinctive – even if borrowed – visibility. That which makes visible is itself brought conspicuously before our vision rather than, as otherwise happens, merely being taken for granted as the condition of vision. In this accomplishment nature can be regarded as imitating art, at least as imitating the mode of painting that, as with the Impressionists, inverts our usual way of seeing: whereas we usually focus exclusively on the things that are visible without taking note of the spread of light that renders them visible, such painting lets us see the light spreading through the atmosphere, sometimes making it especially conspicuous by painting it over the things that in ordinary vision it would make visible. Attentiveness to such scenes as that of the summer snow shining atop the mountains could, on the other hand, prompt one to ask whether, conversely, such art imitates nature, whether it imitates the way in which nature discloses its most elemental moments. Or is there both originality and imitation from both sides, a kind of reciprocal mimesis?

Stretching down the mountainside, as if its darkness contended with the shining on high, the forest is likewise displayed in a way that is contrary to our usual perception of it. On the mountainside we witness it with an expansiveness that would otherwise go unseen. We apprehend it as having density, coherence, and extent by virtue of which it resists being construed as a mere thing or group of things. We apprehend it in its elemental character.

Thus gathering all these elements around it—earth in the guise of stone, water in that of snow, sky with its texture of clouds, the light that comes from the fire of the heaven, the forest in its density and extent—the mountain peak along with the Alpine scene centered on it provides an incomparable site for nature's disclosure of the elemental—especially when brought into clear focus by phenomena such as the summer snow.

Untitled
(Oil and pencil on
paper), 18×24 in.

Untitled
(Oil and pencil on paper), 18×24 in.

11
Dark Light

Seis am Schlern
Südtirol

July

When we speak apart from nature, even in speaking of nature, the lines that separate things, the figures of their demarcation, are distinctly drawn. Light is light, and dark is dark; and if, as at twilight, they appear to blend, it will be said that they do so without either of them relinquishing anything of itself to the other. One arrives, the other withdraws, and it is only a matter of their presence, of the degree of presence of each. When one arrives and the other withdraws, then, as always, light remains light and dark remains dark.

Speech attests, then, that there is no dark light; it rules out decisively the possibility that such a conjunction might occur, takes it to be no less immediately self-vitiating than the concept of a triangular square. Light may grow dim, and the things it illuminates may come to appear only faintly, only indistinctly. Light may, as at dusk, gradually give way to darkness. As night approaches and the surrounding landscape recedes toward virtual invisibility, it is enveloped by both the light that remains from the day and the darkness that, almost imperceptibly, descends upon it. Yet it is as if, in driving the light from the scene, the approaching darkness remains nonetheless distinct from it, the one receding precisely as the other supervenes upon the landscape. Though it is speech that conveys the seal, perceptiveness will also – almost always – concur.

And yet, there are occasions, all too rare perhaps, when dark light is to be seen. Most often clouds serve to bring it into view, for of all the things that let us see light, none let it appear in such various guises as do clouds.

.   .   .   .

Picture a heavily overcast day in the high Alpine valley. Above the entire valley and the mountains surrounding it there stretches a dull gray, absolutely motionless canopy, which passively admits the daylight, as if through a remote sphere, offering nothing distinct or indicative. This entirely uniform cloud cover is cast inestimably far above even the sheer vertical peaks of the Dolomites, which soar more than a thousand meters above the valley. But it is otherwise with the wispy cloud traces, hardly compact enough to constitute really distinct clouds, that float just above the valley. Almost as if lending their motion to the rocky peaks just behind them, they offer a promise of light even on such dark days. It is not that they reflect the daylight nor that, as on sunny days, they capture the light and embody it in their almost – but not quite – insubstantial materiality. It is rather that their soft, light, drifting grayness displays a certain affinity to light itself, simulating in its visible presence and steady flow the largely invisible stream in which light is cast toward the things that it will illuminate. As they not only float before the face of the mountain but also, as if in a kind of slow motion, drift into the deep crevices that articulate and in some cases divide the peaks, these wisps of cloud simulate also the power of light to penetrate wherever there is an opening for it.

Overnight there was a light snowfall in the very upper reaches of the mountain, and now the white covering is especially visible on a less than vertical surface adjacent to the peaks. The look of the fresh snow under the heavily overcast sky brings out, through subtle affinity, the dark light of the clouds. At this time of year there is little chance that the thin coating of snow will survive the day; it will prove only slightly less transitory than the drifting clouds. Because the rock surface still shows through the light covering and here and there juts up through it entirely, its white is not quite the whiteness of snow. Not that it is other than white: there is no trace of color cast across it, not even from the underlying rock surface. It can only be described as dark whiteness, and it is largely on this account that it shows an affinity to the drifting clouds and, like them, simulates light in its very darkness.

In all these sightings of dark light there persists a vision of a scene that, though sighted yesterday shortly after my arrival, remains so vivid that it seems still somehow present. The sky was already fairly heavily overcast, and there was already a hint of the approaching darkness. The cloud cover was relatively low, just above the peaks, and was uniformly gray. But then there came into view a higher, much darker band of clouds; it was as if these darker clouds had spread downward from the top of the dome. This band was distinctly set apart from the lower, lighter band by what looked like a horizon. Then, shortly after it had come into view, the horizon began to move slowly downward so that the band of dark light extended ever farther over the lighter, uniform gray, gradually concealing it and enveloping the entire scene. When, in a matter of minutes, the dark canopy had broadened downward so far that the horizon finally coalesced with the contour of the mountains and the lighter band was entirely dispelled, the landscape below remained dimly visible, as if illuminated by the dark light. This wondrous scene of dark illumination was brief. Soon it began to rain, and the darkness of night, intensified by the clouds and rain, descended over the entire valley. Then one could only imagine the soaring peaks, withdrawn, as they were, into their elemental obscurity.

**Puerta del Sol I
(Sun's Gate I)**
(Acrylic on paper),
18×24 in.

**Puerta del Sol II
(Sun's Gate II)**
(Acrylic and pencil
on paper), 18×24 in.

12
At Sea

Dalmatian Coast
Croatia

August

The ship set out from Trogir. It was a small ship carrying only a dozen passengers and manned by a crew of four. We were to be at sea for a week, remaining on the ship except for relatively brief evening visits to a few of the cities, towns, and other sites along the way. As the ship pulled out of the harbor and headed southeast along the coast of the mainland, its continual swaying and the loud splashing of the waves against its side offered a constant reminder that we were at sea. The sky was perfectly clear, and though it was late afternoon, the sun still felt very warm on my skin. Yet the air had by then grown cooler, and once we had set out, I could feel its cool dampness as it blew across my face.

At sea one is almost completely surrounded by the elements, more thoroughly amidst them than perhaps in any other setting. Open to the sky and to the light that is its gift, one is surrounded by the sea as one looks off to the high mountains of the coastline that can be seen through the slightly misty air. All are there – sky, sea, mist, wind, mountains, as well as the lines where they are conjoined, as the coastline joins land and sea; all are there, not just as things are present, but with a manifestness that touches all one's senses and expands one's very sense of nature. By contrast, when one is on land – except in very remote places – there are always in view things fabricated by humans as well as various other signs of human intervention in the natural world. And when traveling by air in a modern jetliner, one is almost entirely insulated from the elements; and in this setting vision is almost the only sense that remains receptive to them. But at sea, granted the technical, nautical supplement required by humans, there is little else but sea and the other elements around it. Not only can one's vision be captivated by it, but also one hears the pounding of the waves, smells the briny presence of the water, feels the dampness of the sea on one's skin. All the senses, each in its own way, open ecstatically to the sea and thus also to the sky, the air, the mountains, with which it elementally convenes.

The elements display a distinctive, indeed unique kind of singularity. Each is singular – the sea, the sky, the earth – yet their singularity is such that, unlike things, they are to a large degree absolved from individuality. There is only one sky; it is even one and the same sky, and yet it is not something individual, does not have the form characteristic of individual things. There is only one earth, which is always one and the same; though it can be partitioned, separated off from the sea by coastlines, neither the absolutely singular earth nor its partitioned-off regions assume the form of individual things.

The elements are not things, even though since antiquity the view has prevailed that whatever in the natural realm really *is* must be thing-like. If, at sea, one sets such views aside and lets the elements touch one's senses in the most concrete fashion, then the elements can become most strikingly manifest in their singular, encompassing character.

Even the sheer stone of the massive mountain range off in the distance (the Mosor mountain range) displays a certain singularity that a mere stone object lacks; for the stone of the mountains is stone *of the earth,* stone that is still earth, stone the character of which is determined by its being of the earth, in contrast to an individualized, perhaps fabricated, in any case detached stone object. The more purely elemental an element is, the more absolutely singular it is. The most absolutely singular of the elements are earth and sky.

The ship docked overnight at Makarska on the mainland coast and then on the second day sailed around the eastern tip of the island Hvar and on past the ancient city of Korčula. We were bound for Dubrovnik, where we would spend the second night.

What caught our attention as we passed Korčula was the high wall that surrounded it. Originally constructed no doubt to protect the city from pirates or invading forces, the wall was built right at the edge of the sea, its contour matching that of the shoreline, its stone similar – except for its smoothness and regularity – to the massive formation that constitutes the shoreline. Much the same accord between the stone wall and the natural, shore-lining stone would be observed in Dubrovnik. It has always been at locations where the sea borders the land in the most suitable way that coastal cities have been built. Indeed the way in which the sea borders the land determines not only how humans build their cities but also how they live in these cities.

As the ship sailed on toward Dubrovnik, it passed along the southern coast of the so-called half-island Pelješac. Along the entire stretch there were high mountains coming all the way down to the sea, and there were no signs whatsoever of habitation, nor even of human intrusion. Though the mountains were dotted with evergreens and so were less desolate looking than those we had seen along the mainland coast, what appeared most remarkable were the huge stones, their color bordering on white, that ran along the base of the mountains, extending upward for several meters from the water's edge. This horizontal band of stones was completely devoid of vegetation, and thus it served to mark the coastline quite conspicuously. Indeed it constituted the coastline; it was the coastline, thus inscribing the elemental articulation between land and water, earth and sea.

The sea had calmed a bit, and now that its surface was more uniform and undisturbed, more mirror-like, the sparkling of the sunlight became so remarkable as to be nearly indescribable. Such sights evoke, of course, a flood of metaphors that prompt us to imagine seeing dancing figures, sparkling gems, and so on. Yet these come too readily and as mere metaphors fit much too loosely.

The sparkling consists of instantaneous flashes. Each of them – if indeed one can speak here of individual flashes – appears momentarily, and in that very moment it is gone. In a rigorous discourse the word *it* would have to be effaced, for, strictly speaking, there is no "it" that sparkles but only the sparkling. The instantaneity of the sparkling forestalls its taking shape, its coming to have a form or some other determination that could be construed as its essence and perhaps even as the "it" that sparkles. Rather, the sparkling occurs as a sheer, instantaneous coming-to-light of light itself, as light traces.

The ship reversed its course at Dubrovnik and then on the third day of the voyage veered off almost due west toward the island of Mljet. Though morning had brought cooler air, the heat soon returned, and as the ship reached the eastern tip of the island, the cicadas could be heard singing their praise of the intense sunlight. The sea remained fairly calm, and the spectacle of the sparkling sunlight continued until, reaching the western end of the island (celebrated by the ancients for its natural beauty), the ship pulled into the harbor of the village of Pomena. We disembarked for a stroll through the village and in the woods beyond. With the aquatic shinings still very much in mind, the contrast became evident: the instantaneous sparklings on the surface of the water had been much more indicative of the phenomenon of light than the brightly lit spots that were now to be seen on the patches of ground around us. For in the latter case the light is assimilated to the ground so that what one sees is simply illuminated ground. Although the sea, too, can appropriate light, as when it assumes the color of a sunset, the sparklings, these instantaneous, random-seem-ing shinings, are not assimilated by the sea but rather are given back, indeed in such a way that the surface of the sea itself goes unseen. In a flash they are gone without having revealed anything whatsoever of the sea itself. It can be said, of course, that the sea sparkles, but the syntax of the assertion distorts and conceals the phenomenal character of the sparklings. To be sure, the sea pertains to the phenomenon, but not as the agent of the sparkling; it is, rather, that the sea only lends its aid to this bringing of light to light, assists in letting light show itself in and through these traces.

Shortly after our morning departure on our fourth day at sea, the captain shut off the engine and the crew hoisted the sails. For more than an hour the ship was silently propelled along by the wind in the sails. The more concrete, more direct sense of being at sea that was now elicited served to focus attention on the elemental character of the wind. As one experiences the way it fills the sails and drives the ship onward, it becomes ever more manifest that the wind cannot be appropriately regarded by means of the categories derived from things. Not only is the wind elemental, but it is the *invisible* elemental par excellence. One sees it filling the sails only in the sense that one sees the sails being filled yet without seeing anything that fills them. The wind is even more invisible than light: for light can in a way – as in the sparkling traces on the water – become visibly manifest, whereas the wind itself is never to be seen. One sees only its effects, as when it fills the sails. On the other hand, when at sea, one feels the wind almost constantly on one's skin, and one often hears the whistling or howling of the wind. So, despite its invisibility, the wind engages the senses. Furthermore, it often bestows on other forms a kind of voice, lets them sound in such a way that they, along with the wind itself, become audible: as in the rustling of the leaves, in the whistling in the pines, in the crashing of the wind-driven waves.

Early on the fifth day, the ship pulled into a small cove where we passed most of the day enjoying the lovely surroundings and musing over all we had seen of this ancient land. Already by midmorning the cicadas had begun to sing under the intense sunshine, as so

often I had heard them in Greece. The similarities between Croatia
and Greece, both of the landscapes and of the seascapes, could not
but prompt comparison. While there were indeed many similarities,
there was one very striking difference. In Greece most sites – certainly
those most frequented by informed visitors – are linked to events,
institutions, arts, myths that have figured significantly in the course
of Western history and that, even still today, mark for us founding moments that were decisive for the West. In Croatia, on the other hand,
there are few such sites. There are, to be sure, some medieval cities
that retain much of their former character; yet as a land successively
occupied by foreign powers (by Greeks, Romans, Venetians, etc.), there
is scant evidence of an indigenous founding culture extending into
the course of Western history. Here there are no sites comparable to
Athens, Samos, or Ephesus. Or Crete.

.   .   .   .

Only two months ago, in Greece, I had set out with two friends in search
of one such site. It was not a site of anything actual, not a site where the
Greeks carried out some founding endeavor, but rather a mythical site.
The site that we set out to find was a site told of in Greek myth, a site
where, according to myth, an event took place that had to do with the
gods, not with mortals. The place toward which we set out had for many
centuries been identified and celebrated as the site of this event, though
as a mythical site there is no telling what it might mean for it to be cer-
tified as actually this site or even for there to be evidence that it is in fact
the place where the – mythical – event took – is said to have taken – place.

We set out driving from Rethymnon along the northern coast of Crete, past Irakleion, and then headed south on narrow, winding roads through the high mountains. Finally, at a remote location far inland, we came to the Lassithi Plateau, a broad plain relatively lush and green in contrast to the bare, desolate mountains surrounding it. The locals in a small village directed us to the base of the mountain where the foot path began that led up to the point, almost at the summit, where we were to find the Dictean Cave. This was the site–so it was said–where Zeus was hidden away by his mother, Rhea, to prevent his being swallowed by his fearful father, Kronos.

From the mouth of the cave there is a steep descent into the cool, damp, dark interior. Without artificial light one would see nothing once one climbed more than a few steps down from the entrance. When, after the long climb down, one reaches the floor of the cave, one sees a number of statue-like stalactites and stalagmites, which look almost as if they were produced by human art rather than merely by water and stone. Yet they have an unusual look, displaying a smooth, moist sheen; it is the look of a water quite other than that of the sea, a water, rather, of the earth, or rather, of the underearth, a water belonging to the interior of the earth. Otherwise, however, there was little to see that could not be readily seen in other such caves.

It was, then, primarily the connection with myth, the quasi-mythical connection of the cave with the myth, that made the site something of interest. Some more concrete signs could readily be called up: that as light alternates with darkness, so Zeus, sovereign of light and sky, had first to be hidden away in the darkness of the cave; and as Zeus has his domain there above, so the cave opens near the summit of the mountain, opens onto the sky. Yet what makes the fact of such a site perhaps most significant is the affiliation that is affirmed between the mythical and the elemental, hinting, as it does, that the mythical has its source in elemental nature, that it is even a guise – not without disguise – in which elemental nature comes to light.

.   .   .   .

As we sailed on, we arrived, on the sixth day, at a small harbor town, Milna, located on the large island of Brač and directly across from Split. Evening in the town provided an opportunity to witness something distinctively Croatian. It was a musical performance featuring a male chorus and a group of dancers. They were dressed in colorful traditional costumes and offered a lovely performance of Croatian folk songs and dances. The simplicity and freshness of the singing and dancing were exquisite.

On the final day the ship returned to Trogir. We explored the narrow passageways of the old city and visited the twelfth-century cathedral, which was replete with images meant to remind humans of their mortality. Our final hours before our return to northern Europe were graced by a magnificent thunderstorm, still another display of the elements, which we had so often experienced at close hand while at sea.

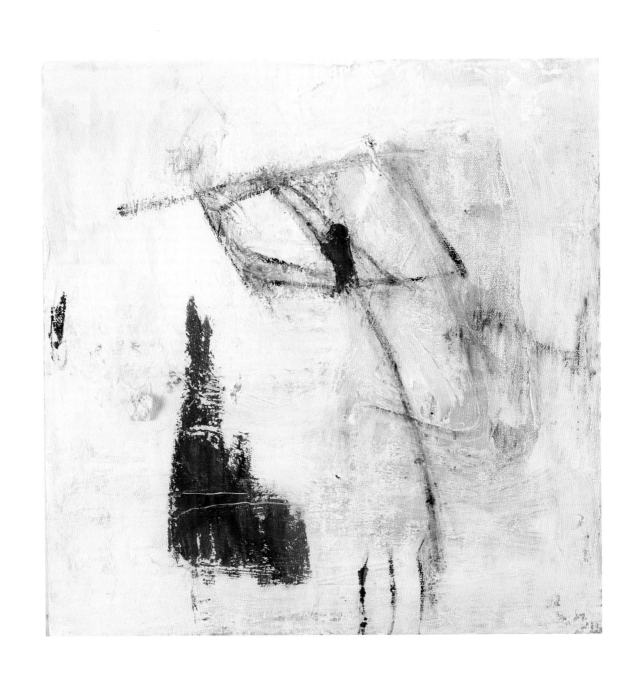

Sailing
(Oil and pencil on
canvas), 12×12 in.

13
Seacoves

Town Cove
Orleans, Cape Cod

Gotts Cove
Georgetown, Maine

August

I went down yesterday to the harbor along with some of my most perceptive friends. We were eager to observe the sea at close hand, to relish the sights it offered, both the sea itself in its various guises and all that was gathered around it or that might emerge from it. As we walked on silently, heading directly toward the landing, past all the spectacles that might have distracted us, we not only anticipated the sights at sea but also were brimming with expectations that being at sea would prompt memories retained from the most cherished tales of the sea. For to us it was no secret that stories often come to round out our experiences, not only adding what they lack but also expanding and articulating their sense.

The small ship that we boarded embarked from Provincetown and headed out toward the open sea. Gradually the outer cape receded from view, and in less than an hour we were out of sight of land.

Once the ship reached the location where at this time of year whales are most likely to be spotted, it slowed almost to a standstill and we waited patiently, though very expectantly, for one of the great creatures to appear. Now the captain had cut the engines, and the ship merely swayed and bobbed with the waves. As I stood on the deck looking out across the open sea, the slight movement of the ship reminded me just how contingent the supportiveness of the sea really is. Even though the water was fairly calm, the gentle rocking of the ship and thus the need to keep one's balance were constant reminders that, unlike the earth, the sea offers no firm stability. In order to cope with the sea's instability, we have recourse to technical supplements, to sailing vessels and all the equipment designed to guide them safely over the uncertain expanse of the sea. But even when by means of a ship a certain support is gained, the sea remains inconstant and destabilizing; it never lets us forget that the support it provides is gained only by technical means and that without those means it would engulf us. To even the most secure vessel the sea remains always threatening. There is the ever-present danger that the sea may overwhelm the vessel, especially when, as in a storm, it concurs with other elements. No matter how secure the ship may be, the sight of land always offers the sailor the promise of security.

The appearance of a whale borders on the indescribable. Breaking suddenly through the surface of the water, the huge creature then immediately dives back into the sea so that its smooth, silky body, glistening in the sunlight, glides in an arc above the surface until finally its great, broad tail disappears beneath the water. It is a sight that can serve to crystallize one of the most remarkable features of the sea. Unlike the earth, which is so closed off that living things can only penetrate or burrow into it, the sea encloses a wealth of living creatures, sheltering even those that must periodically, like the whale, come momentarily to the surface. Furthermore, as openly enclosing, the sea – again, in contrast to the earth – admits the sunlight that strikes its surface, not simply absorbing it and returning it as the color of things, but spreading it throughout, at least down to a certain depth. It is primarily by virtue of this feature that the sea has proven such an apt metaphor for the human condition, for within this medium all are dependent on the gift of light from the openness above, though, within the medium, the light is obscured precisely in being conveyed and can be seen in its purity only in the momentary glance yielded by the utmost ascendancy. It goes perhaps without saying that this metaphorics is also exceptionally open, its terms submitting to various interpretations; it can readily be adjusted along the lines of traditional systems of belief but can also be set, subversively, against such systems.

When one is out at sea out of sight of land, disorientation is almost inevitable. Whereas on land there are nearly always distinguishable things, which, even if unfamiliar, still provide a certain orientation, at sea there is almost nothing capable of giving a sense of direction. All around, the sea looks much the same, and it is only by looking to the sky that a directionality can be determined.

The horizon at sea is one of the most remarkable phenomena. If one focuses on a point on the horizon and then slowly shifts one's vision first to the left and then to the right, the horizon has the appearance of a straight line. The curvature that it must have – since, if one turns

90°, it is still there – is not perceptible at all. This effect can result only from the fact that this line, both separating and conjoining sea and sky, appears without there being anything else against which, in reference to which, its straightness or curvature could be measured. Yet still, the phenomenon is remarkable: it is as if, without having curved around at all, the horizon can nonetheless appear all around! It is perhaps only at sea that this pure horizon, appearing in this peculiar way, violating ordinary geometry, can be observed.

.   .   .   .

This morning I awakened early, still marveling at the visions of the open sea and its inhabitants that yesterday's excursion had offered and that remained vividly in my mind's eye. I made my way down to the edge of the cove, hoping to observe how the sea enclosed by it would receive the early morning light. The broad cove opens onto Nauset Harbor on the Atlantic; from there it extends northwest around Stony Island before turning back almost directly south and reaching all the way down into Orleans. It is appropriately called Town Cove, as it not only reaches almost to the center of Orleans but also separates East Orleans from the Rock Harbor area, almost exactly bisecting this part of the cape.

From the bank just above the edge of the cove, I looked out eastward across the water. Now the pure linear horizon of the open sea had been replaced by the stands of trees across the way on the other side of the cove; as far as I could see from this spot not far from the southern end of the cove, the water appeared to be entirely enclosed by land, though I knew that to the north beyond (and obstructed by) Hopkins Island the cove turned southeastwardly toward the ocean.

The early morning quiet was broken only by the occasional sound of crows. The sailboats and other small craft that later would glide across the cove had, at this early hour, not yet appeared. The sun was barely above the trees on the other side of the cove. The sunlight glistened on the surface of the water, as if it were igniting an array of sparks there across the way. The brilliant, momentary flashes appeared to be leaping from one place to another without traversing the intervening space. At times they appeared to have shafts of light attached to them; then they displayed also a certain verticality, and their ever-changing array became all the more luminous.

It was as if the sparkling surface were a terrestrial – or rather, thalassic – image of the starry heaven. It was also as if each of the points of light, sparkling with such intense luminosity, were a tiny image of their source and the surface of the water a giant mirror in which the sun itself could be reflected. It was as if in these images we could see what we can never look upon directly, what offers us no more than a momentary glance. Yet in their own way the images, too, allude to the limitation, imitate the withdrawal of the source from direct vision: for each point shone only for a brief moment, so that of them, too, only a glance was possible.

As the sun climbed higher, the entire array of sparkles receded across the cove until only a few could be seen. Then it was only a short time before they were gone, as if their brilliance had announced a new day. To be sure, they would reappear occasionally in the course of the morning, but never with the intensity and spread that early morning had given them.

. . .

Now, only a few weeks later, these images continue to gather around the present spectacle, giving it a kind of imaginary or memorial setting. Or rather, here at Gotts Cove in Maine, the spectacles of the open, yet sheltering sea and of the brilliant reception of light at Town Cove provide the mind's eye with scenes of contrast with what here is most striking. Gotts Cove is quite narrow and extends only a few hundred feet before it runs out into a broad bay that, in turn, opens onto the Atlantic several miles to the south. Within the cove itself, which is narrowly enclosed by the banks and partly shaded by tall trees, there is the utmost contrast with the broad, open expanse of the Atlantic. A luminous spectacle not unlike that seen on Cape Cod could indeed be seen out on the bay in early morning, and a certain progression of the brilliant flashes could be followed as they moved across the bay and into the cove.

Most striking, however, was what I observed when, around midafternoon, it began to cloud up. It was not that individually discernible clouds came rolling in or even just took shape. Rather, the sky simply underwent, almost imperceptibly, a gradual alteration, its uniform blue slowly mutating into an equally uniform gray, while simultaneously becoming ever darker. Fog began to appear across the bay, eventually enshrouding completely the forest on the other side. All the differentiations of color, except for that of the nearby landscape, gave way to complete uniformity as all blended into the same dull gray. Then the sparks and flashes that adorned the water's surface in the early morning light had vanished; on land as well as on the water, nearly all traces of light and shadows had disappeared, as if light itself had withdrawn into the monochromatic gray of the sky. Now the sea and the sky had become exactly the same color, a color that was little more than just lack of color. Now that the equally gray fog had rendered invisible the line of trees on the other side of the bay that in the bright morning hours had marked the boundary between sea and sky, this boundary was completely effaced. The horizon had vanished entirely, and sea and sky had coalesced into an expanse of dull, undifferentiated gray. It was as if the scene served to announce – in advance and with an emphaticalness that only such days provide – the withdrawal of light that would come with nightfall.

14
Sunspots

Boston

September

They come and go with the clouds, fading into the surrounding shadows as the clouds come to block the direct sunlight, disappearing entirely whenever the clouds are sufficiently dense, then reappearing as if by magic. If they appear on the forest floor, then some of the growth that is sparsely spread across that expanse is also illuminated, its shiny leaves sparkling in the same light that casts the sunspots. If the clearing comes right after a severe thunderstorm, then the growth and the grassy areas adjacent to the forest glisten all the more radiantly, almost as the surface of the sea, in direct sunlight, sparkles so brightly that it itself becomes virtually invisible. For light not only illuminates things but also conceals them, shelters them with a glistening veil; the more intense the sunlight becomes, the more impenetrably the veil is spread before them, and the more insistently they refuse to yield to our vision. Yet they hide, not as in a darkness that would enshroud them, but rather in brightness so abundant that it glazes them with invisibility.

Not only the cloud patterns but also the configuration of treetops are responsible for the sunspots. Yet, if simply observed, these creatures of light appear autonomous, as if coming and going by their own will; they expand or shrink, they grow brighter or dimmer, and they shift their position, alter, if only slightly, their location, within the entire configuration.

Although the leaves above may glisten in the sunlight, indeed in such a way that the delicate drops of water retained from the recent rain become visible, the space between the treetops and the sunspots on the ground below remains completely devoid of the light, untouched by it. Cast through the treetops so as to project the sunspots on the ground below, the light remains – except at the extremes – entirely invisible. It cannot be seen in this space, though the sunspots attest unmistakably that it must stream down, if invisibly, through this space. Only on the ground, in the appearance of the sunspots, does the light become visible. It is as sunspots that what makes all things visible is itself made visible. So much, at least, do sunspots have in common with painting, that they make visible the invisible vehicle of visibility.

As cast by the invisible light beaming down from above, the sunspots make manifest an enigma at the very heart of visibility, a counterpoint that virtually sets nature against itself: that what makes all things visible has such a capacity to remain invisible, as though invisibility were its natural state and visibility the rare exception.

Sunspots also have much in common with the appearance of things, with the way in which things show themselves. For just as there are sunspots only within the pattern they form with the surrounding shadows, so likewise things appear only against a shadowy background. Never does a thing appear in its entirety all at once. Never can it be seen simply as a whole. All that actually appears, all that can be directly seen, is a single face of an object, the face seen from the perspective of the observer, the face that faces the observer; all the other faces that could be seen remain in the shadows. If the observer alters the perspective from which the thing is seen, then one of the other faces appears; but then the face previously seen will have withdrawn into the shadows. An additive process by which all the faces would be gathered into a single appearance is thus precluded.

The thing in its entirety is both seen and not seen. At any moment one face is actually seen, and everything else is filled in by means of expectant imaginings of what will or could be seen and retentive adherence to what has been seen. Hence, time itself, the expanse of time, comes to ensure the persistence of the shadows that frame everything we see.

It has been said that in absolute brightness one sees just as much and as little as in absolute darkness, that pure seeing is a seeing of nothing, that something can be truly seen only in darkened light or illuminated darkness. In this respect sunspots are like the visible, like the things that can be truly seen; for sunspots are precisely areas of light that are surrounded by the darkness of shadows. To those who are sufficiently perceptive, these sparkling gems set in darkened light are subtle reminders of how we humans engage and are engaged by all things.

A few weeks from now the sunspots will no longer be there. Though they will not simply have disappeared, they will have stretched out into long bands of light, indeed to such an extent that their former designation will no longer be suitable. They will also have receded, will no longer stand out from the shadows as they did a few weeks earlier. Once most of the leaves have fallen, the shadows cast by the bare limbs across the fading green of the field will have become more prominent. It will be as if what were once sunspots had been stretched entirely out of shape by the shadows. The once brilliant disks of light will have become mere indistinct, inconspicuous bands, as if drained of their former vitality by the lengthening shadows. In these as well as other displays, light portends the advent of winter.

But then, several weeks later, with the first snowfall, the sunspots will reappear more brilliant than ever, letting the soft, yet intense whiteness of the snow appear. Around the snowy sunspots the configuration of shadows cast across the uniformly white surface will image the pattern of the heavily laden branches above. This at least is the sight that will be seen when, on the morning after the snow, the new day brings a cloudless sky and the crisp, clear air that bestows on all things a unique, purer visibility. Then the light of the winter sun, low in the sky even toward midday, will filter obliquely through the snow-covered branches, passing almost invisibly until, reaching the ground, it becomes visible in the sunspots.

Templo I (Temple I)
(Acrylic and pencil
on paper), 18×24 in.

Templo II (Temple II)
(Acrylic and pencil
on paper), 18×24 in.

**Templo III, Entierro
(Temple III, Burial)**
(Acrylic and pencil
on paper), 18×24 in.

15
Visible Time

Boston

October

Not many leaves have yet fallen. Most are still green, even if beginning to show fringes of orange and yellow. Yet there are already a few trees that have donned their fall colors, displaying them brilliantly on days that are bright and clear, attesting visibly to the arrival of the season. Though the sun now stays a bit lower in the sky and the character of the light is noticeably different from that of summer, there is still, on bright, clear days, more than ample sunlight to let the blaze of color appear in all its radiance. Though the light itself seems more transparent than ever, the shining of color that its presence releases is unmatched by any other that nature has to offer. With the arrival of these bright, clear autumn days, it is as if the glorious yellows, oranges, and reds had been held in store throughout the summer, as if they had been carefully prepared by nature to announce the advent and then the progress of the new season. Within a couple of weeks the color will have reached its high point, and only the evergreens will have escaped nature's brush entirely. Yet by then the leaves will also have begun to fall.

To be sure, fall is not immune to dark, rainy days, though in the earlier weeks of the season they typically are far outnumbered by the bright, clear days with their almost silver light. When the days are overcast, the bright colors not only are muted but also seem to withdraw into whatever green is still around, almost as if reenacting in reverse the transition from summer to fall. Or else they appear to recede in favor of the dull brown of the dry, ever-clinging oak leaves, portending the seasonal transition still to come.

But for now the spectacle is that of fall as it approaches its peak. The treetops with their still abundant foliage sway in the breeze, their leaves like miniature sails driving the branches to and fro. The breeze is gentle, with as yet only the tiniest hint of the fierce, frigid winds that winter will bring. In the woods the ground vegetation is still fully intact, though only some of the sturdier bushes still retain the full green of summer. Already the ferns, in particular, those most ancient inhabitants of the woodlands, show signs that they will soon don the crisp, beige mantel that sees them through the winter. Thus they – and indeed the spectacle at large – display their light traces of the progression of the season. All serve to render time visible.

There is an ancient view of time that regards it as essentially apart from nature, as having its origin, instead, in the human psyche. According to this view, neither past nor future can *be* except as sustained within the psyche, for the past is what is no longer and the future is what is not yet. Past and future – and hence time as such – can *be* only insofar as presence is bestowed on them, in the one case by memory, which renders the past present, and in the other case by expectation, which renders the future present. Thus, time originates in and through the operations of memory and expectation, and consequently it has its originary locus in the psyche. Without these psychic operations there would be only the punctual *now,* the temporal character of which would be dissolved by its severance from past and future. Whatever is displayed as temporal beyond the psyche, for instance, the progression of the day and of the seasons, must, then, according to this view, be regarded as no more than a derivative, secondary temporality projected upon nature. Time itself would have nothing to do with the earth and its display of the abundance and desolation that are brought by the seasons, nor with the sky and its display of the passage of the day and of the alternation of day and night.

This view has persisted since late antiquity but has all too seldom been put into question, despite the visible manifestness of time with which nature surrounds us. For in its unfolding, nature bears the past with it, as in the case of the summer green that is still displayed on the leaves that now, in early fall, are fringed with orange and yellow. Conveying its past into the present, nature effects an operation not unlike that of memory. Similarly, nature's present has present within it the future, as, for instance, in the orange and yellow fringes now shown by the leaves that in a couple of weeks will be entirely ablaze with these colors.

If the imperative today is to forgo setting the psyche quite apart from nature, then neither can originary time be set entirely apart from the visible time shown by nature. If, furthermore, it turns out that the elemental bounds of human life are composed as temporal – in the form of natality and mortality – then it will be imperative also to ask how these temporal forms belong together with the time displayed by elemental nature.

16
Wild

Woods near Boston

November

Although the day was overcast with a thick, steely gray cloud cover, the deep orange of the bird's breast – a color not unlike that of a robin – shone almost as on a bright summer day. This coloring, along with the distinct white bands on the feathers of its broad, fan-shaped tail, made its specific identity nearly unmistakable. But the dark red patches on its shoulders, which, when it was in flight, broadened to form much of the leading edge of its wings, served to dispel all doubt. The bird was a red-shouldered hawk.

When I first noticed it, the huge bird was on the ground, stirring up the crisp, brown leaves that at this time of year form a thick covering on the floor of the woods. The hawk had come as if from nowhere; and having most likely caught a glimpse of a mouse, chipmunk, or other small creature amidst the leaves, it had alighted momentarily on the ground. Then a moment later it had flown up to a branch of a nearby tree, and there it sat, its majestic posture matching perfectly the superior height from which it surveyed the woods all around. Gripping the branch with its sharp talons, it sat perfectly upright, its tail feathers extending below the branch. For a long time its body remained completely still as it swiveled its head almost full circle, an exemplary model of a creature utterly attentive to everything around it. I noticed how the end of its beak curved slightly downward and how this feature made the hawk appear all the more ready to swoop down to the ground, should some small creature suddenly come into sight. The bird's eyes were fixed, and yet its stare was intense. As with most wild things, they had that strange look, that uncanny remoteness, that, once one has experienced it, leaves no doubt but that a chasm separates humans from living things that are truly wild. This unbridgeable separation across which genuine communication is virtually impossible—however delightful and even significant birdsongs may be to us—is not an indication of rank or superiority, for it is all too evident that in many respects the capacity of wild creatures such as the hawk far exceeds that of humans. Though there are of course many affinities that we have with wild things, affinities that we can grasp with some assurance, the difference that separates us from them, perhaps attested most strikingly by the eyes of such creatures, is such that all our concepts fall short of it. At best, we can get a glimpse of the wildness in the eyes of such an animal and can acknowledge on the basis of this experience that wild things are irreducibly other.

After remaining for some time with its body completely motionless, the bird suddenly, with a hop, turned half circle and then resumed its stance, surveying the woods in the other direction, maintaining exactly the same posture as before. One could of course compare the hawk's action to that of a sentinel or a hunter, and up to a point such comparisons would not be inappropriate. Yet assimilation to concepts both geared to humans and formed by them must be critically inter-rupted if one is to remain true to the experience of wild things and, above all, to the look of wildness in their eyes, to what their look reveals, or rather only shows in its utter remoteness. If, as has been said, the eyes of humans are – for other humans – the windows of their souls, then it needs to be said of wild things that through their eyes they are, at once, both exposed and utterly withdrawn, that in their look there is brought to light a presence that is, at once, no more than a trace. In the look of – and from – its eyes, the wild animal itself is not presented, but its presence is merely traced; it is presented as withdrawn from presentation, presented as not present in the look as we apprehend it. There is no match between our sensibility and the wild look in the eyes of such a creature.

. . . .

It may seem that the wildness of such creatures is something left over from an earlier nature, that it is a remnant of nature in the form that prevailed before the assault to which it is now subjected was launched. No longer is there need to discern and interpret signs of this assault, for what was once only foretold, first as an ideal for humanity and then, later, as the greatest danger, has now become actuality, indeed an actuality that draws everything, including all human interests, to itself and turns against whatever is posed beyond its scope, assaulting the alien, banishing the other. While advanced technology with the resources it provides for altering the natural course of things (for instance, for communicating across a distance without actually traversing that distance) is requisite for this actuality and its assault on nature, it is not simply technology that produces the monstrous consequences that now become more and more apparent. Rather, technology only opens up the possibility of the assault for which nature would be no more than a source of materials and energy; also, however, it opens other possibilities, possibilities of supplementing or directing the natural course of things. For actualizing the assault there was required a political-economic complex that, appropriating technological resources, promoted the assimilation of all things both natural and human to the endless round of ever-increasing production and consumption.

To preserve wildness in the wake of rampant capitalism will become ever more difficult. That wilderness areas, established in the effort to preserve wildness, mutate all too rapidly into tourist sites is an index of the difficulty. Yet perhaps nothing is more imperative for catching a glimpse of what lies outside this debilitating uniformity. That there are things in nature that by their very nature resist assimilation attests to a break, a fissure, in the armament of the present complex. There is every reason, then, to celebrate creatures like the red-shouldered hawk whose wildness will yield to nothing short of utter destruction and extinction.

.   .   .   .

After a short while I looked up again toward the branch that had served as the hawk's lookout post. The bird was gone. It had slipped away, had quietly flown back into the woods, perhaps to return tomorrow, perhaps never to be seen again. Such is the way of wild things: that they come as if from nowhere and then, after a time, again slip away.

Guerrero (Warrior)
(Acrylic and pencil
on paper), 12×18 in.

17
Quiet

Countryside near Boston

December

Now, after the snow, there is not the slightest hint of the wind that so recently swept out of the northeast, bringing with it the first winter storm of the season. Now the trees and everything around them are completely still. Not even the slightest breeze comes to give voice to the dry, brown leaves that still cling persistently to the branches of the oaks. There is not the slightest rustling among them. Only silence.

Yet it is a silence to be heard. Indeed it is heard all the more keenly because the present scene continues to be touched by that of the fierce snowstorm, not as something called up and actively remembered, but as continuing on its own to flow into the present, enduring without the slightest effort on our part. Touching the present scene ever so slightly, framing it from beforehand, the scene of the howling wind and driven snow still resounds. It is a scene that continues to hover before our eyes, letting us still sense almost palpably the power of the storm, its power especially to make visible the otherwise unseen pliancy of the trees, their capacity to endure the onslaught of the storm. The scene of the storm is a past borne along in the present, still visible in the scene that now lies before us; the flow of past into present–of time itself–is gathered into the scene after the snow.

But now, after the storm, all is quiet. The heavy, dark cloud cover remains, making the pure whiteness of the snow seem, by contrast, to shine all the more brilliantly, lending both intensity and shape to the otherwise dark light. Even if sounds were to intrude on the silence, the tread, for instance, of someone walking across the snow, almost nothing would be heard; for the snow cushions and absorbs all that sounds, quiets whatever might come to break the silence. While we know that the quiet will not last indefinitely, we hold at bay the moment when disruption will inevitably come, project it effortlessly into an indefinite future, opening thus a protective interval between the present scene and the disturbance to come, an interval that prevents that future from touching the scene that now lies quietly before us. While bearing the memory of the storm–or rather, letting it be borne along by the present scene–we hold in suspension all expectation of what is to come. At least, this is what we are required to do if we would experience the quiet of this scene.

Now all remains still. No animals, not even the birds, have yet ventured out into the new world that has been crafted by wind and snow, these lightest of the elements. Wild things, too, remember in their own way what has happened; their acute senses trace the altered contours, and they remain cautious. One could imagine that the scene is that of a painting, to which time and motion could not properly belong, were it not for the clumps of snow that occasionally turn loose and fall from the trees. Yet as they fall they dissolve almost into snowflakes, as if reenacting in reverse what happened during the storm. By the time they reach the ground, they have dissolved into a spray of powder. The silence goes unbroken. All remains quiet.

The quiet calls for quiet, for silence, for listening in silence to silence, and, when they come, for words infused with silence. It calls for words whose hushed borders enclose a deferral of sense, a waiting for what is to be heard only by listening to the silence. What can come to be heard will perhaps eventually be said, spoken, openly sounded; but nothing does more violence to the silence than the prematurely sounded word. Indeed the word *silence* itself exemplifies this exigency: to say the word, except silently, is to break the silence.

A few days from now, warmer winds will likely arrive, and the thaw will begin. Though at first imperceptible, the thaw will soon alter the smooth, powdery look of the snow's surface. Small streamlets will appear here and there, but most of the melt will be absorbed by the ground. If the warmer weather holds, patches of earth will begin to show, attesting once more to its persistence through all changes. For a time, the earth will hold the memory of the snow, displaying it in the dampness that remains not only to touch but also to sight. We, too, will retain its memory, yet ever more passively, as we are quietly drawn away to other days and other concerns.

Winter I
(Oil, pencil, graphite,
and charcoal on
paper), 18×24 in.

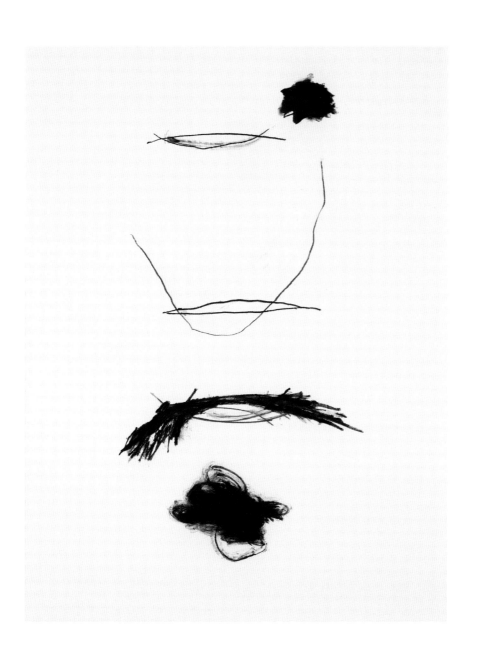

Winter II
(Oil, pencil, graphite, and charcoal on paper), 18×24 in.

Winter III
(Oil, pencil, graphite, and charcoal on paper), 18×24 in.

Winter IV
(Oil, pencil, graphite, and charcoal on paper), 18×24 in.

Winter Traces
(Oil and pencil on
paper), 18×24 in.

18
White

Boston

January

Some days have passed since the big snowfall. It was a gentle snow with large snowflakes coming straight down, as there was almost no wind to divert them or to set them whirling about. Indeed, it was less like a storm and more like a dreamy, magical scene, almost as if staged purely for our enjoyment and in this sense exemplary of natural beauty. As the snowflakes floated slowly downward, they were the very picture of lightness itself. At the same time, they brought light to the scene, which otherwise was darkened by the heavy overcast that had foretold the arrival of the snow. Even when the snow picked up and became so thick that it obscured everything in the distance, it still conveyed a brightness to things nearby, enhancing their visibility while letting everything else recede into virtual invisibility.

The snow lasted for a full day and night, and when on the next morning it had finally stopped, everything in sight was covered, snow clinging even to the bare branches that, as the clouds cleared away, were silhouetted against the bright sky. Soon the sun reappeared, and then the sky shone more purely and intensely blue than perhaps at any other time of year. It is at such a time, under such conditions, that the whiteness of the snow attests most radiantly to its elemental affinity with light. For white is almost light itself. Hardly anything differentiates them except that light is invisible as such, that it becomes in a way visible only when it strikes something and makes that thing visible; white, on the other hand, gives back the light, reflects all that the light harbors and so is itself eminently visible. Yet despite its harboring all colors, white is itself hardly – if at all – a color. It makes exceptional demands on the painter, who cannot on his canvas exploit the resources of shading; for there are no shades of white, as there are shades of blue and yellow. There is only white itself, and even what is quite similar to it is nonetheless off-white, not a shade *of* white. With some painters, such as Cézanne, it is as if sometimes they simply give up, abandon the effort to paint white, and so just let the bare white canvas serve this purpose. Perhaps the only thing of this kind that requires of the artist still greater skill is carnation, the color of (a certain) human flesh, a color that, like white, is not simply a color but that harbors all the primary colors, without merely blending them.

On the other hand, white need not be simply uniform in its appearance. When, in the light of the low winter sun, the trees cast their shadows across the surface of the snow, patterns of light and dark appear there. Lacking a continuum of shades, white breaks up into areas that are differentiated by the contrast between bright and dark. It is this kind of differentiation that the painter must exploit in order, with white, to fashion on the canvas something more than a mere undifferentiated white surface.

Painters have observed that in white all colors disappear; they remain so thoroughly harbored by it that they do not appear at all. In the visibility of white, all other colors remain invisible. Thus, Kandinsky regards white as representing a world where all colors have disappeared; and from such a world – one might add – virtually all things, too, would have disappeared, except perhaps for something like a pure, uninterrupted expanse of snow. In any case, Kandinsky's conclusion is that since such a world is utterly remote from us, white affects us like a great silence; we hear white just as we hear, for instance, the silences that composers insert in their music as momentary interruptions of the development of musical content. Harboring all colors and their respective sounds, white is like a receptacle anterior to the beginning.

The snow, too, as it settles over all things, altering or concealing their shape, lets the world appear in another light, lets it seem more remote. The snow also brings silence, as even humans huddle indoors and for the moment suspend their noisy comings and goings. Yet they have only to step quietly and attentively into this magical white world in order to learn to see in a new light and to listen to silence.

JOHN SALLIS is Frederick J. Adelmann Professor of Philosophy at Boston College. He is author of many books, including *Logic of Imagination: The Expanse of the Elemental* (IUP, 2012), *Transfigurements: On the True Sense of Art* (University of Chicago Press, 2008), *Topographies* (IUP, 2006), and *Force of Imagination: The Sense of the Elemental* (IUP, 2000).

ALEJANDRO A. VALLEGA is Associate Professor of Philosophy at the University of Oregon. He trained as a visual artist before studying philosophy. He is author of *Sense and Finitude* (SUNY, 2009) and *Latin American Philosophy from Identity to Radical Exteriority* (IUP, 2014).